The
GOOD ASSEMBLY

INFANT ASSEMBLIES

CLAIRE DERRY • JOANNA PITKIN

Scripture Union
130 City Road, London EC1V 2NJ.

List of contributors

Practical Guidance for Assemblies: Issues to consider by Claire Derry, Primary Schools worker (Lancashire) for Scripture Union

Esther Bailey (21, 34)
Claire Derry (1, 2, 3, 4, 5, 6, 11, 12, 13, 14, 15, 18, 20)
Helen Franklin (35)
Rev Stephen Holroyd (stories for 4, 26)
David Lewis (script for 6)
Ann McFiggans (follow up assembly 4, and outline 16)
Joanna Pitkin (7, 8, 9, 22, 24, 25, 26, 27, 28, 29, 31, 38, 40)
Richard Powell (23, 41)
Maggie Reid (37)
Julie Sharp (sketches for 1, 19)
Helen Thacker (ideas for follow-up work)
Helen Venables (17, 29, 30, 32, 33)
Elaine Weaver (36, 39)
Lorraine White (10, 31)
Christine Wright (stories for 7, 8, 9, 28, 40)

© Claire Derry and Joanna Pitkin 1994
First published 1994

ISBN 0 86201 909 5

British Library Cataloguing-in-Publication Data. A catalogue record for this book is available from the British Library.

Phototypeset by Intype, London
Printed and bound in Great Britain by The Bath Press, Avon

Contents

Practical guidance for Assemblies
Class-led assemblies

Practical guidance for Assemblies: issues to consider

A school aiming to provide an assembly for every school day of every year, needs to invest a lot of time in preparation. At a time when pressure on teachers is so great, it is understandable that a school's assembly programme does not always come top of the list of priorities. In my experience, a useful assembly book is one which a teacher or other adult can pick up and in it find ideas which spark the imagination and creativity of the person using it.

This book has been compiled to include some class-led assembly outlines and some teacher-led outlines. However, I hope it will also be useful to those other people, including clergy, parents, and schools workers, who may be invited into schools to take an assembly from time to time.

Practical guidance

Whilst recognising that preparation time is often minimal, planning the content and structure of an assembly is very important and the time given to this is often reflected in the end result!

Even if the assembly is not being led by a class, it is very valuable to involve the children corporately or a few volunteers, as it helps to hold the children's attention. Young children obviously have a fairly short attention span and this can be affected by a variety of things. Assembly is not always held at the start of the day and it can be very hard to hold the attention of, and to communicate well with a reception child at the end of a long day at school. It can also be difficult to relate equally well to a four year old and a seven year old in the same assembly.

Some schools are short of space, and children are often squashed quite tightly together in order for everyone to be present. The length and content of the assembly must take these things into consideration and the person leading the assembly should be flexible.

Perhaps there have been times in the past when the content of infant assemblies bore little relevance to the lives of the children. Today we realise that it is important to see assembly within the context of the whole curriculum, the life of the school and the child's experience outside school, while at the same time making it a special and separate event. Assemblies that complement or even emanate from other things in school are often the most meaningful and valuable ones.

In my experience, assembly can change the mood or atmosphere throughout the school. For this reason alone, the planning and practical considerations surrounding an assembly are worth the time and effort.

Important points for visitors taking assembly

1　However the invitation to take assembly has come, as visitors you must work to gain credibility and respect in the eyes of both the staff and the children. There are usually many opportunities to help in school with this age group. If you can take the time to be a helper on a school trip, or mix paint, or hear children read, it can make all the difference. Then you will have spent time with the children and had some contact with the staff.

2　There may well be a certain amount of 'healthy suspicion' towards visitors at first. However, a well thought-out and carefully prepared assembly will allay any fears that you are only there to gather new church members.

3   It is essential that you know what normally happens in an assembly. This may mean attending an assembly beforehand and finding out about duration, format, topics being covered, music, etc.

4   If as a visitor you wish to lead some singing but can't play an instrument it may be possible to liaise with a teacher at the school who can help. Perhaps the teacher could practise the song you wish to include with the children beforehand. If you do choose to teach a new song yourself the following steps are a guideline:

a) Sing/play the whole song right through to the children.

b) Sing/play line 1 – the children repeat it.

c) Sing/play line 2 – the children repeat it.

d) Sing/play lines 1 and 2 together – the children repeat the two lines.

e) Sing/play line 3 . . . follow this sequence until the whole song has been learnt.

5   Find out if there will be children from other faiths present and/or children with special needs. Remember this when planning the assembly.

6   It is important to show concern and sensitivity to what is currently happening in the school. It may be that a child has had a serious accident that week or someone has won a dancing trophy etc.

7   In an assembly try and communicate just one point and do this in a variety of ways.

8   Prepare thoroughly beforehand and take time to have several 'trial runs'.

9   Arrive with plenty of time to spare and keep to the time given.

10 Always dress smartly, be polite and courteous to the staff and show respect for each child, never embarrassing them in front of others.

11 Once a school knows and accepts you, why not ask if it would be possible to take a series of assemblies?

This may lead to a greater impact than the occasional 'one off' assembly.

Issues to consider

The way assemblies are viewed, their purpose and aim, varies tremendously from school to school. This book contains outlines which are of a specifically Christian nature and does not draw on the teaching of other religions. Nearly all the outlines are based on a particular Bible passage or on broad traditions of belief which are shared by all Christians. However, the outlines aim to be relevant and interesting to those children who are not from Christian backgrounds. It is hoped that by drawing on Christian teachings the children will think about their own attitudes, values and actions, and be allowed to develop spiritually.

The outlines also seek to comply with the advice given by the DFE in England which requires that broadly Christian worship
a) must contain an element related specifically to the traditions of Christian belief;
b) must accord some special status to Jesus Christ;
c) must not be distinctive to any particular denomination;
d) must contain elements common to Christianity and other religions.

When thinking about the issues surrounding assemblies it is essential to remember that all children must attend unless their parents withdraw them. We must therefore act with integrity and respect towards the children, allowing them to respond in a way that is appropriate to them, never pressurising them into particular beliefs. We must think most carefully about the attitudes we convey and the language we use, never abusing our captive audience. This is important with all ages but perhaps most especially with infants who take things so literally, and are usually so eager to please.

Opposites

1 Wise and foolish

Adult led

Aim
To help the children see that following Jesus involves listening to his words and obeying them.

Bible base
Matthew 7 v21 and v24–27. Christians listen to the teaching of Jesus in church, from others, when they read the Bible and when they pray. They try to turn what they have heard and read into practice! Christians say Jesus' rules are good ones to 'build' your life on.

Preparation
Collect together simple props for the story. Props could include: two woolly hats labelled Fred and Bill, 'toy' tools, two plastic spades, two kagouls, an umbrella, and some wellington boots. A teacher may wish to ask two older children or mature Year 2's to run through the sketch a few times beforehand, the children miming the appropriate actions. It is possible however for another adult leading assembly to pick two children to do the actions there and then in the assembly. You may wish to ask if it is possible for the children to learn/ practise the following songs: 'Don't build your house on the sandy land' and 'The wise man built his house upon the rock' (*Junior Praise 1*).

Presentation

Talk to the children about their homes, asking particularly if there is anyone living in a newly built house or flat or living near to where new homes are being built.

Discuss the first stages of building a house. Explain clearly exactly what foundations are, and say why there needs to be level ground, deep and strong foundations, etc. Talk about the disaster there would be if building rules were not kept to. Discuss other rules the children know of at school – in the classroom, in the playground. What happens if the rules aren't kept? Stress the positive side of rules, for example, if the school rule was 'Think about others first' and everyone did, what kind of school would you have 'built'?

Jesus told a story to help us see that obeying his words or his 'rules' is the best way for us.

Introduce the 'Fred and Bill' sketch.

Once upon a time there were two men. They both wanted to build themselves a house.

One of the men was young and wise.

Some people thought he was too careful.

Some people thought he was too fussy.

His name was FRED. (*Put on hat.*)

He had a good idea about the sort of house he wanted to build.

He wanted it to be quite tall, quite wide.

He wanted it to have a window at the front, a door at the back.

(*On the words tall, wide, window, and door perform actions to suggest these. For example reach up high with both arms to suggest tall.*)

He looked around for a good place to build.

He looked all over the country.

He walked up high hills looking for a place to build.

He walked by the sea.

He walked through jungles and forests. (*As he walks*

10

in these places Fred mimes walking up a hill, by the sea and through jungles and forests.)

Sometimes the ground was too muddy and he sloshed around in his wellies (Wellingtons).

Sometimes the ground was uneven and there was nowhere flat to begin the foundations.

Eventually he found just the right place.

He had a wonderful view for miles around and the land was solid rock.

He asked his friend if he could borrow a hammer, a drill, and a very strong spade and he hammered and he drilled and he dug until he had made a deep hole in the rock. (*As he hammers, drills and digs give Fred the appropriate tools to mime these actions.*)

Then he put 54 wooden struts, lots of bricks and a specially strong cement into the hole to make VERY STRONG FOUNDATIONS. Then Fred built his house, quite tall, quite wide, with a window in the front and a door at the back.

He settled in quickly. He tidied up his garden, put in a few tomato plants and was happy. (*Fred pretends to build his house.*)

Fred had a friend whose name was BILL. (*Put on hat.*)

Bill wasn't too clever but he also wished for a new house.

He had very grand ideas. He wanted . . . 7 floors, 100 windows, 33 bedrooms, 4 dining rooms, 2 kitchens, 8 bathrooms, *and* an indoor swimming pool.

But Bill didn't care much about the land.

He bought the first piece of land for sale that he saw.

As he walked across it his feet sank into the squelchy mud, but he just thought it would make it easier to build.

He dug down a few centimetres and then started building the walls.

He didn't care about digging deep, or making strong

foundations. (*Bill mimes walking on squelchy ground, digging and building*.)

In just a few weeks he had a magnificent mansion with 7 floors, 100 windows, 33 bedrooms, 4 dining rooms, 2 kitchens, 8 bathrooms *and* an indoor swimming pool.

He moved in straight away.

After Fred and Bill had been in their houses a few days a terrible storm blew up.

The wind howled (owoo), the lightning flashed across the sky, the thunder roared and worst of all the rain lashed about the houses.

Fred put on his kagoul, his boots, and got out his umbrella.

He went out in the rain to check the house was all right and his tomato plants were standing up.

Then he went back into his house, shut the door, made himself a cup of tea, and settled down to watch TV (or mention the latest "in" programme).

Bill was lying in bed when something started to drip on his head . . . he got up quickly.

Soon the drip had become a stream and he had to leave the room altogether.

He quickly burrowed around in his wardrobe for his kagoul.

He had to leave the 7th floor because of the flooding, then the 6th, then the 5th, 4th, 3rd, 2nd, 1st . . . until finally he had to run out of the house altogether.

He stood there in the horrible mud looking at his house.

First the ceilings caved in, then the walls fell outwards.

The first floor collapsed into the swimming pool until . . . finally the HOUSE FELL FLAT! Bill stood there in the pouring rain looking at the ruin of his beautiful dream house.

*funnier *Better ending

But Fred, who had been careful and wise, not too full of wild ideas and who didn't mind spending extra time finding the right place to build, was safe and dry in his house built on rock. When he looked out of his window he saw Bill standing crying by his ruined house and he rushed out with his umbrella to ask him to come in.

After the sketch ask the children questions about the story, eg Why did Bill build on the mud?

Emphasise again how important the strong foundations were. Talk about how the things Jesus asks us to do (his words) are like those foundations. Christians believe Jesus' words are the best ones to follow and obey if we are to be like Fred the wise man. Sing 'Don't build your house on the sandy land' or 'The wise man built his house upon the rock'.

Class work
* Design your ideal house.
* Look at different types of houses.
* Visit a building site and discuss the different materials used for building. Which are the best and why?
* Play a 'beetle drive' game but build up a house shape instead of a beetle. A six must be thrown to start the foundations.

The following books are based on the Bible story:
The House on the Rock by Butterworth and Inkpen, (Marshall Pickering)
The Two Houses (Little Lion)

2 Lost and found

Adult led

Aim
To show the children that Jesus loves and cares for each one of us.

Bible base
Luke 15 v1–7. The story of the Lost Sheep.

Preparation
Made/bought puppet of a sheep, three fairly large outlines of sheep with the words **Who** in one, **is** in one and **Wensleydale?** (or other appropriate sheep name!) in the other, four cards with the letters **l o s t** printed clearly on them, and a few party hats, streamers, etc.

Presentation

Welcome the children to assembly and ask them if they have noticed any lost sheep around school. (*Have the three sheep outlines stuck up around the hall/room a little hidden if possible.*) Choose three volunteers to find these and bring them to the front. Move the children around so the sheep make the question 'Who is Wensleydale?' Read this together. After a few suggestions reveal your pet sheep (the puppet) who will help you tell a story. Ask the children to help with the story by responding with a 'baa' sound every time they hear the name 'Wensleydale' and to shout 'Hooray!' each time the 'Good

Shepherd' is mentioned.

Story with puppet and responses

Move the puppet appropriately as you tell the story of the Lost Sheep (Luke 15 v1–7) using the name Wensleydale (or another) for the sheep who wandered off along the lane, past the orchard, over the stile and into a thick dark clump of trees.

As you tell this part of the story, invite the children to give you the initial letter of these places and choose children to come and hold these letters up (*use the four cards prepared earlier*). Spell out together the word these letters make.

Emphasise that poor Wensleydale was **lost**! Tell the children how much the Shepherd loved and cared for the sheep. He was prepared to leave the other 99 to go out looking for just one who was lost. As you tell how the sheep is found, brought home and friends invited for a party, invite a few children to help you celebrate at the front. All the children could join you in singing to the tune of Happy Birthday, *Welcome home Wensleydale, welcome home Wensleydale, You're safe in the sheep fold, welcome home Wensleydale.*

As this is happening the hats can be worn by the children out at the front and at the very end they can throw the streamers!

Discuss together why Jesus told this story, showing the parallel between the shepherd's love and care for the sheep and Jesus' love and care for us.

Use the song 'Have you seen the pussycat' (*Junior Praise 1*) to reinforce this.

End with a prayer if appropriate, thanking God for his love and care for each one of us.

Class work

* Ask the children to close their eyes and think of something special. Then ask them to imagine that they lose

it. Encourage them to talk about how they feel about losing it, eg angry, upset. Ask them why the thing they thought of was special and what they would miss about it. Then ask the children to imagine finding it a few weeks later. How do they feel? The children could then write their own stories and poems.

* Further 'lost and found' stories in the Bible – The lost coin (Luke 15 v8–10), The lost son (Luke 15 v11–31).
* Personal safety – Don't go with strangers.
* Shepherds in Jesus' time and now.
* Different breeds of sheep, the wool process, and general sheep farming.

Year 2

* Activities using the number 100.
* Design a maze.
* Wool pictures.
* Knitting!

3 Rough and smooth

Adult led

Aim
To help the children consider that quarrelling and jealousy in families makes God sad.

Bible base
Genesis 25 v27–34 and 27 v1–28.

Preparation
A box (with a hole in the top big enough for a child's hand) containing objects with different textures for a 'feelie' game. Props for telling the story: a will, a flask of lentil soup, fur, etc.

Presentation
Try to wear something with an interesting texture to it, eg corduroy, angora wool, velour. Begin by discussing with the children the feel of things they are wearing. Move on to discuss the texture of other things around you in the room. Then explain that they will now play a 'feelie' game. You will secretly place objects in the box, some with a smooth texture and some with a rough texture, volunteers will come out to the front, place their hand in the hole in the box and, just by feeling, try and guess what the object is.

Story

Tell the children that today they will hear the story from the Bible about two brothers, one who was born with hairy skin and the other with smooth! Explain that in Jewish families the older son would get twice as much of the family fortune when the father died as the younger one. Use the props to tell briefly how Esau, the older son, gave up this privilege to Jacob his younger brother, in exchange for a bowl of soup! (Genesis 25 v27–34) Go on to tell the children the story from Genesis 27 v1–28 of how Jacob tricked Isaac their father by wearing an animal skin and pretending to be Esau.

Talk to the children about times at home when they are jealous of brothers and sisters and about quarrels they have had. What could they do about being jealous? How could they stop the quarrels? Remind them that God understands but that it makes him sad. Discuss the love and forgiveness that is needed in families and how they can be grateful for all the things they have.

Perhaps say some 'sorry' prayers.

Class work

* Continue further with the story of Jacob and Esau explaining how Jacob runs away and doesn't come home until years later (Genesis 33).
* Learn the rhyme 'Esau and Jacob' (*Let's Join In*, p 30).

4 Little and large

Adult led

Aim
To help the children cope with bullies and also times when they feel inadequate.

Bible base
David and Goliath. 1 Samuel 17. David has been secretly anointed king by Samuel, rather than any of his seemingly more suitable brothers. His brothers join the Israelite army but David remains a shepherd boy taking care of his father's flock. One day he is sent with food for his brothers to where the Israelite army are fighting the Philistines. David, still a young boy, but confident in God's strength, stands up to the Philistine giant Goliath, who is taunting the Israelites.

Preparation
Prepare beforehand a life-sized picture/collage of Goliath, nearly three metres tall!

Presentation
Talk to the children about times when someone bigger than they are has tried to push them around and make them do something they don't want to. For example, if someone isn't being very nice they might come up and say, 'Give me your bike or I will beat you up!' We call that sort of person a bully. Introduce the story with the

large picture of Goliath.

Goliath was almost three metres tall — now that is *really* big! That is probably three or four times as big as any of you. Goliath was very strong and fierce. He had big, strong hands to fight people with, and great strong legs to run after people with, so they couldn't run away. Now I don't know about you, but I think I would have been a little frightened of such a big man. But not only was Goliath big, he also had a very big sword for cutting people's heads off. Because Goliath was so big, he went around bullying people. As soon as he saw something that he liked, he would lean over and say, 'Give it to me or else!' Goliath was a bully.

Goliath had lots of not very nice friends. They were the Philistine Gang. They wanted to push all the people in Israel out of their country, and take the whole country for themselves. It was just like someone coming up to you and saying, 'Give your house to me or else!'

Now, all the people who lived in Israel were frightened and they did not know what to do. They sent their army to meet the Philistine Gang, but then great big Goliath appeared. He would stand in front of the army and say, 'I dare one of you to come and fight me! You can't beat me. And when I win you must give your country and everything you have, even the clothes that you stand up in TO US.'

Well, all the people in Israel were *so* frightened of Goliath and the Philistine Gang, they just stood there with their knees knocking, and their teeth chattering. They were *so* frightened.

Now if we are really honest we know that we would be frightened if a big gang and a giant came and shouted at us, wanting our toys and our clothes.

So what were the people who lived in Israel going to do about this big bully Goliath and the Philistine Gang? What sort of things would you do? They could have tried saying NO loudly to make Goliath go away. Can you say NO loudly?

They could have run away, but Goliath and the Philistine gang would have run after them and caught them.

They could have got someone to run off and get some help. Do you think that would have been a good idea? But no one in the country of Israel knew what to do.

They didn't say NO. They didn't run away. And no one thought of running off to get some help. They were just in a knee-knocking, teeth-chattering mess.

But, help was on the way. I wonder if you can guess who was coming down the road to where the people of Israel had their camp? It was just a young boy, carrying some cheese sandwiches for his big brothers who were there with the rest of the people of Israel.

It was David. When he reached the place where all the people of Israel were standing with their knees knocking and their teeth chattering, he asked his brothers what was going on. They told him all about the Philistine Gang, and the three-metre-tall Goliath. David said, 'I don't know why you are so afraid. Don't you know that God is on our side?' You see, God is always on the side of people who are being bullied.

David's words were heard by the king and he called David before him. To start with, David could hardly understand the king because even the king's knees were knocking and his teeth chattering. The king said to David, 'You're only a boy. What can you do about big Goliath and the Philistine Gang?' David replied, 'Look, your Majesty, I look after my dad's sheep in the fields and on the hills. When big bears and roaring lions come I have no one to help me, only God. He gives me the strength to shout at them and even to fight them.'

The king was impressed by David's bravery and his trust in God. He put his armour on David so that he could go out to fight big Goliath: iron trousers, an iron coat and an iron hat. They were all so heavy that David kept falling over. David said, 'Forget the armour, your Majesty, I won't even take a sword. I shall stand up to this big Goliath because I feel safe with God as my friend.'

So David went out to meet Goliath with just his shepherd's stick and his catapult. The closer David got to him, the bigger he looked, but David was not afraid, he knew God was with him. Goliath looked down at this young boy and said, 'Go away, I don't fight midgets. Hang around and I'll squash you.'

But David did not run. He felt safe because he *knew* God was with him, even though he could not see him. He just looked up at Goliath and said in a very loud voice, 'NO! YOU GO!' Then he shouted, 'I've got God on my side, you've just got those weedy Philistines.'

At this, Goliath decided he had had enough. He got out his big sword and charged at David. The ground was shaking under David's feet as Goliath charged down upon him but David knew he was safe. He took out his catapult, put a small stone in it, whirled it around his head five times, then let the stone go. It hit Goliath right in the centre of his forehead with a loud thwack. Then there was an even louder crash as Goliath fell to the ground.

David had won. All the people cheered David as Goliath fell. Now their knees were no longer knocking and their teeth were no longer chattering. Now it was the Philistine Gang who were frightened and without big Goliath they decided to run away.

It was good for the people of Israel that David came and helped them deal with the big bully Goliath and the Philistine Gang. When we face bullies who try and take things from us, like our toys and sweets, we do not have David around the corner, but we must not be like those people of Israel who did not know what to do.

Goliath as bully

Talk with the children about bullies and how to respond. If we feel safe we must say NO loudly to a bully. If we don't feel safe we must run away and not just stand there with our knees knocking and teeth chattering.

We should go and tell someone who can help us and remember that God is on our side.

Finish the assembly with a prayer, thanking God that he is always with us.

Appropriate songs to include are: 'God is for me.' (*Cry Hosanna*); 'Only a boy called David.' (*Junior Praise 1*).

Class work

* Various measurement activities including finding the smallest and tallest person in the class, in the school, using non-standard and standard units of measurement.
* Look at catapults in relation to work on 'forces'.
* Look at different sorts of armour through the ages.
* The following idea could either be used as an assembly or class work to follow up the story of David and Goliath.

Preparation Make a large Guy Fawkes character.

Presentation Show him to the children and explain that you are going to build up his name.

The first letter is B – for big, he is one of the biggest boys in his class.

The second letter is U – because he can be unkind to smaller children in the school.

The third letter is L – he often laughs at people and makes fun of them.

The fourth letter is also L – when the teacher asks him if he's been naughty he lies and blames someone else.

The fifth letter is Y – is this like you?

For each of the letters talk to the children about how that person would make you feel.

5 Storm and Calm

Class led

Aim
To help the children realise that God is in charge of everything, even the weather!

Bible base
Mark 4 v35–41.

Preparation
Props for the 'Guess the weather' game: sunglasses, umbrella, woolly hat and scarf, etc.

Mime shivering and putting on hat and scarf, then ask the class to guess the weather. Invite the class to come up with their own ideas for props or simple actions to represent different types of weather.

Choose several children to do their actions for the weather in the assembly. Memorise the story from Mark 4 v35–41 in a simple form choosing three key words to which the children will respond with a certain noise or action. For example, wind *ooh*, waves *woosh*, rain *splish splash*. The children from the class leading the assembly could be divided into three groups: wind, waves, and rain. In each group one child could play a percussion instrument (chosen by the children) to represent their sound while the others in the group just make the noise when the appropriate word is used. Practise all this with the children beforehand.

Presentation

Talk to the children about the weather on the day of the assembly and then introduce the 'Guess the weather game'. Children from the class leading the assembly walk across the front wearing various items and/or miming an action to represent different types of weather. The other children must guess what the weather is.

Perhaps make the last one some type of 'wet' weather to introduce the Bible story of the stilling of the storm. Explain to the children that you want their help in telling the story. Every time you say the words *wind*, *waves*, and *rain* (or which ever words and sounds you have chosen) they are to say, just twice, *ooh*, *woosh*, or *splish splash*. Let the three groups from the class give a demonstration and use them to lead the others.

In your telling of the story emphasise the fact that Jesus cared for his friends and helped them, and that the wind and the waves obeyed him and stopped.

Talk about how we can't control the weather and that it is only God who is powerful enough to be in charge of it. The weathermen/women can tell what it will be like a little way ahead, but they cannot change anything.

Talk about how God, who is great enough to control the weather, cares about each of us and can help us when things are difficult, just as he helped the disciples.

Sing 'With Jesus in the boat' (*Junior Praise 1*).

Class work

* Discuss the many different types of weather and how they affect people in various places in the world.
* Let the children paint pictures or symbols of their favourite weather conditions.
* Learn some of the weather symbols.
* Do some weather experiments.
* Read *Miles and the Weather Bureau* by Taffy Davies, (Scripture Union).

6 Greedy and generous

Class led

Aim
To show the children that Jesus wants to be our friend whatever we are like.

Bible base
Luke 19 v1–10. The Story of Zacchaeus. Jesus visits the home of Zacchaeus, a tax collector for the Romans. After this meeting Zacchaeus completely changes. He gives back the money he has cheated people of, in fact, he gives them back *four* times as much.

Preparation
Find a small puppet to be a 'Mean Monster' or draw one on an OHP acetate. Collect together a few simple props to use while the children mime the story and you narrate using the script. Rehearse this with the children.

Presentation
Introduce your Mean Monster to the children. Explain to them that Mean Monster is very greedy, especially with money. Sometimes he cheats people and deliberately steals from them. Probably because of this, he is very unpopular and hardly has any friends. No one ever pops in to see him or brings him a present on his birthday.

Tell the children that in the Bible story they will hear

today there is a man who is a little bit like Mean Monster, but Jesus wanted to be his friend. Explain in simple terms Zacchaeus' job as a tax collector.

The children mime as you read the following script:

Zacchaeus collected taxes for the Romans but he cheated everyone. He was small and fat and everyone called him 'Titch' behind his back. Although he grew richer and richer, he had no friends. This made him very sad.

Zaccheus and a pile of money. People laughing at Zacchaeus. Zacchaeus all alone. Zacchaeus looking out of window.

One day he saw lots of people hurrying out of the town. 'Where are they all going?' he thought. 'Perhaps there's a circus or a fair coming to town.'

He rushed outside. 'What's happening?' he called. 'Go home, Titch,' the people said, 'Jesus is coming and he won't want to talk to you.'

Zacchaeus rushing outside. Crowd turn away from Zacchaeus and walk away.

But Zacchaeus followed the people. There were crowds around Jesus, and Zacchaeus couldn't see a thing. He tried crawling between their legs. He tried jumping up and down. Then he had an idea. He saw a tree and up he went like a fat squirrel, puffing and blowing.

He follows.

Zacchaeus crawls through legs and jumps. Zacchaeus looks up at tree and climbs.

Everyone laughed at him. When Jesus reached the tree, he stood still and looked straight up into the branches.

'Zacchaeus, come down,' Jesus said. 'I'm coming to your house today.'

Zacchaeus couldn't believe his ears! He came down so quickly that he took the skin off his knees!

He felt ten feet tall as he walked along the street with Jesus. He opened his front door and said, 'Please, Sir, come in.' He closed the door. Zacchaeus and Jesus had a secret talk together and they became friends. Zacchaeus felt sorry for all the wrong things he had done.

Outside the people jumped up and down. They couldn't see Jesus now. 'What's happening?' they shouted. Suddenly . . .

Zacchaeus came out with a big smile all over his face. 'Don't go,' he called out. 'I'm going to give half my money away and if I've stolen any money from any of you I'll pay you back four times as much.'

'Hooray, hooray, good old

People laugh. Jesus and crowd look into tree.

Zacchaeus coming down the tree.

They walk together. Jesus and Zacchaeus at house.

People jumping up and down.

Zacchaeus comes out of house. Zacchaeus gives out money to amazed people. Crowd cheer.

Zacchaeus!'

Talk to the children about how Zacchaeus felt when Jesus wanted to come to his house and about how Zacchaeus changed. Remind them that Jesus still wants to be friends with everyone, no matter what they are like.

Sing together 'Come down Zacchaeus' (*Someone's singing Lord*) or 'Everyone in the whole wide world' (*Junior Praise 2*).

7 Class work
* Look at different sorts of money – foreign and British.
* Discuss as a class ways in which the children could share the things they have (eg, toys, sweets, money).
* Perhaps collect money for Children in Need or another charity.
* Watch *The Cheat's House* from the video *Luke Street and Follow the Leader* (Scripture Union).

7 Hungry and full

Adult led

Aim
To show how Jesus can make a lot out of what people give him, and to explore the theme of sharing.

(Similar assemblies on the theme of small actions making a difference are *The Enormous Marrow* and *Friendship Cake*.)

Bible base
John 6 v1–15. The feeding of the five thousand. Jesus and his disciples wanted some time alone when a huge crowd arrived to see Jesus. Instead of sending them away, Jesus spent time teaching them. Afterwards Jesus fed the hungry crowd with some loaves and a few small fish given by a boy. The crowd tried to make Jesus king after this incident.

Preparation
Make some small sandwiches to go in a lunch-box.

Presentation
Start off by showing the children your lunch-box and examining what is inside. Start to share the sandwiches round, but of course they run out. Explain that in today's story something rather different happened.

The children could make sound effects at various points in the story: for example, tapping feet for steps as people arrive, whispering to show the 'chatter' level of the crowd getting louder, then quiet as Jesus starts to teach, rumble-rumble as the crowd gets hungry, munching as they eat.

Sharing a picnic

It was a sunny day.

'If you hurry,' said Jamin's mother, 'you will catch up with Jesus. He's gone in a boat, but you could run around to the other side of the lake and see him again.'

Jamin was delighted. 'Good,' he said. 'I like listening to what Jesus says.'

'You'd better take something to eat,' said his mother. 'I know you. You're always hungry.'

She quickly packed five little rolls of bread and two cooked fish into a basket. 'Hurry,' she told Jamin. 'Keep with everyone else. Don't go off alone.'

So Jamin hurried. Crowds of people had just the same idea and were walking out of town to go around the edge of the lake. Bobbing about far out on the water was a boat. Jamin knew that Jesus was in it and he watched carefully to see where it would land.

It was a long walk, and everyone was glad when they saw where Jesus was going to come ashore. Jamin made sure that he was near the front of the crowd as the people moved forward to see Jesus.

Jesus welcomed them all. When he began to speak Jamin put his picnic basket on the ground and listened. The time went by quickly. When Jesus had finished telling the crowd about God, Jamin was surprised to see that it was nearly the end of the day. Suddenly he felt empty inside. He was not the only one! All the families, who'd been listening to Jesus, now began to rub their tummies hungrily.

Jamin picked up his basket and was just about to eat his first small roll, when he noticed that no one else had anything to eat. The others had come from home in such a hurry that they'd forgotten to bring any food!

Jamin heard some men, the friends who travelled with Jesus, asking Jesus what to do.

'They are all hungry,' said one of them, who was called Andrew.

'Shall we send them away now so that they can buy food from the towns nearby?'

Jesus said, 'Give them some food yourselves.'

Andrew and the others looked worried. 'What does he mean?' they asked each other. 'We haven't a crumb of bread, let alone enough to feed all these people.'

Jamin looked at his five rolls and two fish. It was only enough for one boy, not nearly enough for such a big crowd, but he decided to offer it to Jesus. He went forward.

'I've got this,' he said, pushing the basket up towards Andrew. 'It's not much, I'm afraid.'

Andrew smiled. 'Thank you,' he said. 'Jesus will know what to do. He cares about people being hungry.'

The boy watched as his picnic basket was taken to Jesus. He saw how Jesus lifted out the bread and fish and held it in his hands. Then he thanked God for the food and broke each roll and both the fish into smaller pieces.

The people began to sit down in large groups on the grass while Andrew and Jesus' other friends took the pieces of food from Jesus and handed them round. Jamin had a share too. He ate until he was full.

How could it have happened? Jamin couldn't think! His picnic had been just enough for one boy. Now more than five thousand people were all eating until they were full! There was even some left over – twelve basketfuls of crumbs that no one could manage to eat.

'It must be as Andrew said,' Jamin thought happily. 'Jesus cared that the people were hungry and knew just what to do.'

Sharing *small things*

Talk about the boy's generosity and his willingness to share. It was only a small action but it made a big difference to the crowd.

Class work

Talk with the children about what it means to share sweets, toys, games etc.

Hold a sharing party where everyone brings a contribution and no one is allowed to help themselves but must wait to be served.

Explain that Christian children might be taught about the importance of sharing, about how Jesus can make a lot out of what people give him even if they do not have much to give.

Other resources are *Lion Story Bible no. 36, Five Loaves and Two Fish* (Palm Tree), 'The Hungry Crowd' on *Luke Street and Follow the Leader* video (Scripture Union).

8 Ungrateful and thankful

Adult led

Aim
To show how Jesus cared for those whom others did not like. To think about thankfulness and acceptance.

Bible base
Luke 17 v11–19. Ten men with leprosy are healed. Normally Jews would have nothing to do with Samaritans. Leprosy must have broken down these barriers for there was at least one Samaritan in this group. People who suffered from leprosy were ostracised from the community. The action of Jesus enabled them to return to their homes but only one, the Samaritan, came back to say thank you.

Preparation
The children could prepare pictures for a story roll. On a roll of lining paper, large pictures are drawn depicting the story. As you tell the story, the paper is unrolled to reveal the next picture.

Preparation
Ask the children if they have ever felt lonely. Who helps them? Whom can they help? How would it feel to have no friends, no one to care about us? That is how the ten people felt at the beginning of this story.

Tell the story from Luke 17 v11–19 using the story roll

prepared by the children or by getting some of the children to act it out. Alternatively, use this story:

Matthan was unhappy. He had not been happy since the day when he'd found some nasty red patches on his skin.

'Oh dear,' said his wife. 'You have a terrible skin disease. Whatever shall we do?'

At first, Matthan hid the disease, but before long his neighbours found out why he always covered his arms and legs.

'You have a terrible skin disease,' they told him. 'Don't you know that you must live outside the village now? If you live near us, we might get the disease too. You'd better go quickly.'

Matthan went to say 'goodbye' to his wife and his children. They cried because they knew he might never live with them again. From then on, Matthan had to stay out of every town and village.

'Perhaps,' Matthan thought as he left his own village and set off along a rocky lane to the hilly countryside, 'perhaps I might get well one day. Then I'd be able to go to the priest. He'd look at my skin and say that I'm really better. Then I could go home.'

Yet he didn't think this would really happen. His skin disease hadn't gone after one year, nor even after two years. Matthan began to think he'd never go home.

Instead, he joined other men who also had the terrible skin disease. At night they would sleep wherever they could find shelter. In the daytime, they would go and beg for food. It was a sad life.

Then, one day, everything changed.

'Have you heard of Jesus?' one of Matthan's friends asked.

'No', he replied. 'Who is he?' he asked.

'He teaches people about God,' the friend told him. 'I saw him once. I couldn't go near of course, but I stood behind the crowd around him. I saw and heard it all.

Jesus says God loves everyone.'

'Even us?' asked Matthan. 'I hope he does. Nobody else loves us. Wherever we go people turn away.'

'Jesus seemed to love everyone,' the friend said. 'He even helped those who were ill. He made them well.'

Matthan wished he could see Jesus. 'If only we could ask him to help us,' he said.

'I heard he was coming here,' the friend told him. 'If we go and stand in the lane near the village, we might catch a glimpse of him.'

The two friends walked down the hillside together. As they went they saw other men with the same skin disease.

'We're going to see Jesus,' Matthan told them. 'Will you come with us?'

So, a little later, ten ragged men, Matthan and nine others, were waiting by the side of a dusty pathway.

After a little while, Matthan's friend called out, 'There he is! That's Jesus, the one in front!'

A small group of travellers had appeared in the distance.

'He might not notice us,' Matthan said. 'He might take another path. Let's call out and ask him to help us.' He shouted, 'Jesus, Master, be kind to us!'

They knew that Jesus had heard them, but would he stop and talk to them? Not many people would.

'Jesus, Master, be kind to us!' they begged.

At last, they saw that Jesus had turned towards them. The shouting stopped.

It was quiet as Jesus said, 'Go and show yourselves to the priest.'

The ten men looked at each other. The ugly sores were still on their skin, but Jesus had told them to see the priest, just as though they were completely well!

'Shall we go?' asked Matthan's friend.

'Of course,' Matthan replied. 'Jesus told us to.'

As they walked away from Jesus, on their way to the

priest, an amazing thing happened!

'My skin is smooth and brown!' Matthan said joyfully. 'I'm better!'

'So am I!' exclaimed his friend. 'And so is everyone else.'

Matthan was so happy. He turned round and ran back to Jesus, falling at his feet with joy.

'Thank you, Jesus,' he said. 'Thank you for making me well.'

Jesus smiled. 'But where are the other nine?' he asked. 'Weren't there ten men whom I made well?'

When Matthan looked around he saw that he was alone. The other nine had gone without stopping to say, 'thank you'.

'I'm pleased you came back,' Jesus told Matthan. 'Go home to your family. You are well.'

Talk to the children about why you should say thank you. When do they say thank you, to whom and for what? Is there anything they would like to say thank you for now?

Class work

* Talk further about saying thank you. How does Mum feel if we forget to say thank you? How can we say thank you in actions? Christians say thank you to God when they talk/pray and go to church. What do you think they say thank you for? Look at some prayers from a children's prayer book. Use the books *Thank you for...* (Lion publishing) to trace the idea of a chain of thank yous, eg loaf of bread ... mum, shopkeeper, lorry driver, baker, miller, farmer, God. This idea is also suggested for the Harvest assembly on chocolate.

* Think of all the people in school to whom we could say thank you. Design and make thank you cards for them.

9 Tears and smiles

Adult led with class help

Aim
To show the contrast in feelings at the beginning and end of the story of Jairus' daughter.

Bible base
Mark 5 v22–24, 35–43. Jewish mourning customs were loud and emotional. Hired mourners would have been common amongst richer families. The story is full of contrasts: the despair and unrestrained distress of the mourners compared with the hopefulness and serenity of Jesus.

Preparation
Prepare some cards with the words *A time when I felt sad (happy, excited, afraid etc)*. Ask the children to pick one out and see if they can think of a time mentioned on the card which they could share with the others.

Presentation
Some of the class could start by sharing about the times when they felt happy/sad etc.

Show a drawing of a person with a mouth made out of a red shoelace or wool. Initially the corners of the mouth are turned down so that the person looks sad. Ask the children what things make them sad.

Explain that at the beginning of today's story people

were very sad because a little girl was ill. Tell the story from Mark 5 v22–24, 35–43.

Jairus, an important Jewish leader, seeks Jesus' help for his dying daughter. The little girl dies and the mourning begins whilst Jairus is away asking Jesus for help. When Jesus arrives he sends the mourners away and brings the girl back to life.

As you tell the story, children could take the various parts and wear hats labelled with the appropriate names: Jairus, Jesus, servant etc.

Jairus' daughter

Jairus heard his wife calling, 'Come quickly. Rachel is very ill!'

Jairus hurried into his house. He had been walking along the narrow streets of the small lakeside town in which he lived. Suddenly he was afraid. His little girl was so ill that she couldn't speak to him.

'Poor Rachel!' he whispered, stroking her hot face. She had been ill for a few days, but now she was worse.

'We've tried everything,' Rachel's mother said. 'What can we do? If only Jesus were here again. Do you remember how he made people well when he was in our town?'

Jairus stood up. 'Jesus is here,' he said excitedly. 'When I was out walking I heard people say that he is coming across the lake in a boat!

'Please go and fetch him,' said Rachel's mother. 'Ask him to come quickly. I know he'll be able to help.'

Jairus ran out of the house into the street. He went as fast as he could, but before long he had to stop. The narrow street was *so* crowded with people going to see Jesus that he couldn't run. He pushed and pushed, moving little by little towards the lake.

'I must get to Jesus,' he thought. 'Nothing will stop me.'

The crowd was getting thicker. Soon Jairus was fighting to squeeze his way through.

'I must find Jesus,' he thought. 'Rachel needs him.'

At last, Jairus caught sight of Jesus between the heads of those crowding around him. 'Jesus!' he shouted.

The people let him through. They knew Jairus. He was an important man in the town. He threw himself at Jesus' feet saying, 'My daughter is very ill. Please come to my house and touch her so she'll get well.'

Jesus wanted to help. 'I'll come,' he said and turned to follow Jairus home. It seemed that the whole crowd wanted to come too, and it was even more difficult for Jairus to push his way through. And he was in such a hurry! He knew that Jesus must see Rachel soon or she'd die.

Then, to his surprise, Jesus stopped to talk to an old woman. Jairus wanted to rush Jesus on, to get him quickly to his house. He could hardly keep still as he watched Jesus speaking kindly to the bent, old lady.

Before Jesus had finished, some of Jairus' friends pushed their way through to Jairus. They looked sad.

'Don't bother Jesus any more,' they said. 'Rachel has died.'

Poor Jairus! All that rushing and pushing had been for nothing. He looked up at Jesus, wishing that he'd been quicker.

'Don't be afraid, Jairus,' Jesus said. 'Just carry on trusting me.' Then he called out to the crowd. 'Don't follow any more. Let me take Jairus home.' He called to Peter, James and John, his friends, to come too.

When they arrived at the house, they found some women outside, weeping and wailing because Rachel was dead.

'There's no need to cry,' Jesus said, but the women didn't believe that Jesus could help, so he sent them away.

Jesus and his three friends went inside with Jairus. After the noise and bustle outside, it seemed quiet. Rachel was lying on her bed, very still and silent. Her mother was crying.

Jesus spoke softly. 'Little girl, get up.' He took her hand and she sat up and looked around.

Her father and mother gasped. Rachel had been dead, but Jesus had brought her back to life. They were so surprised that they didn't know what to do or say.

As Jesus went away with his friends he told them, 'She'll need something to eat.'

Jairus and his wife quickly found some food for Rachel, and then they began to smile and laugh, hugging each other for joy! How glad they were that Jesus had come!

Talk about the change in people's feelings, eg from tears to smiles, sadness to happiness. Turn up the corners of the mouth on the picture and ask the children what things make them happy.

Class work

* Other resources which may help are *Lion Story Bible Series no. 45, Becky gets better* (Palm Tree), *The Little Girl's House and Jesus and a Little Girl* (Bible Society), or *The Leader's House* on *Luke Street video* (Scripture Union).

* Talk further about what things make us happy and sad. Who cheers us up when we are unhappy? The children could draw smiley faces, or those that look happy one way up or sad the other way up, or a sad face with a smiley face hiding beneath a flap.

* Explain that Christian children might be taught at church that Jesus cares and has the power to heal. He can bring happiness out of sad situations.

* The children could make two masks for a character in the story, decorating one with a happy face and one with a sad face. The children then take it in turns to wear each mask and say why they feel happy or sad. For example, Jairus: sad because of the death of his daughter; happy because she is alive.

10 Light and dark

Adult led

Aim
To explain that Jesus said he was 'The light of the world'. The assembly *Follow that star* is also on this theme.

Bible base
John 8 v12. Jesus the light of the world. In Bible times people, like today, were very dependent on light. Lamps were used in the temple, in the home and also in marriage ceremonies. The word light was also used to denote life, welfare and guidance. When Jesus used this analogy they would have felt its importance. Jesus was claiming to be the light of truth and the light that guides.

Preparation
Props needed: different types of light, eg candles, gas lamps, torches; also blindfolds and obstacles.

Presentation
Ask for a volunteer. Blindfold them and ask them to move around some obstacles, eg cones. Then ask them to do it a second time with another child helping them. Talk with them briefly about which they preferred and why.

Talk to the children about fears of the dark and how they might be overcome. It can be very frightening when you cannot see around you. It makes all the difference when you put the light on. How do they feel when that happens?

Think together of all the different types of light. How and why are they used? eg candles, lighthouse, torch. Show them some examples.

Jesus said that he was like a light. He said, 'I am the light of the world.' In the same way that light can guide you in the dark and show you where you are, Christians believe that Jesus guides people to do the right things.

Class work

* Read *Can't you sleep little bear*? by Martin Waddell and Barbara Firth (Walker books).
* Talk about symbols connected with light in the Christian church, eg advent candles, Christingle oranges, candles given to babies when they are baptised.
* See the assembly outline *Things that worry us* as a follow-up to fears about the dark.

Friends

11 Determined friends

Adult led

Aim
To help the children realise that we all need friends – friends we can trust and friends who will help us.

Bible base
Mark 2 v1–12. The paralysed man. People were desperate to hear Jesus teach. News of his power to heal had also spread far. Four men bring a paralysed man to Jesus, confident that he can make him well. The Pharisees secretly condemn Jesus for blasphemy as he forgives the man's sins. By doing this Jesus is making himself equal with God. In Jewish law God alone had the power to forgive sins. But Jesus knows what they are thinking and goes on to prove his authority to forgive things by physically healing the man.

Preparation
Cut out four strips (approx. 30 cm long and 4 cm wide) from brightly coloured card. Attach these together to make one longer strip using three paper fasteners. This should give a jointed effect to the strips. Practise moving the strips into the following shapes: a square, a house, steps, a bed (see diagram).

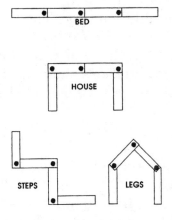

BED

HOUSE

STEPS   LEGS

Presentation

Rush into the assembly carrying a whole armful of things, dropping them as you make your way to the front. If no one helps you to pick things up ask a few children to help. Discuss different times when we need help: when we have lost something, when we don't understand our work, when we fall over. Talk about how important our friends are at those times and the help they can give us.

Explain to the children that the man in the story they are about to hear needed a lot of help from his friends because he couldn't walk. He was paralysed in his legs. Encourage them to imagine what it would be like if their legs and back were so stiff they couldn't move. What would it be like if they couldn't go anywhere unless someone carried them?

Use the jointed strips to tell the story from Mark 2 v1–12, making a flat bed shape, a house, the steps, lowering the bed down, and finally legs that work, bending at the knee and running and jumping.

Bring out of the story how determined the friends were to get the man to Jesus and how sure they were

45

that he could make him better.

Learn together and then sing, 'The Busy Little House' by Ian White (*Songs for Children*).

Ask the children to think of ways their friends help them. Sum up the children's thoughts in a 'Thank you' prayer, asking that we will all learn to be helpful friends for others.

Class work

* Descriptive writing about friends. Bring in photos for discussion/display.
* Look at the types of houses in Israel – why do so many have flat roofs? What are they made from? Why do they only have small windows?
* Find out about a charity directly connected with the physically handicapped.
* Discover how easy it would be for someone in a wheelchair to get about school and your local shops. Are there ramps, disabled toilets, etc? Get the children to think of ways to improve the school environment for a disabled person.
* Read the story *Emma* by Christine Wright (Scripture Union) about a day in the life of a girl in a wheelchair.

12 Forgiving friends

Adult led

Aim
To help the children realise that God wants us to be friends who will forgive, just as he has forgiven us.

Bible base
Matthew 18 v23–34. The Parable of the Unforgiving Servant.

Jesus tells the story of a servant who owes a king millions of pounds. The debt is cancelled because the king feels sorry for him but the servant immediately goes out and threatens a fellow servant who owes him just a few pounds. The king is told about this unfair act and the servant is scolded for his lack of mercy and is then punished.

Jesus uses this story to remind us of how much God has forgiven us and therefore how we should forgive others.

Preparation
Find a broken toy and a football to take into assembly and make up a short story (a modern equivalent of the parable of the unforgiving servant) to tell the children. For example, Steve borrows Mike's new pocket computer game and ruins it, but Mike forgives him. Ian borrows Steve's football and loses it. Steve won't forgive him.

Props for the story: a crown and cloak for the king

and two caps for the servants.

Presentation

Begin the assembly by discussing with the children situations where their friends might have let them down, eg if a friend borrowed a toy and broke it, or played with someone else at playtime. Talk about what they would do, how they would feel, what they would say.

Tell the children your made-up story, showing them the broken toy and the football. Talk about how the characters reacted and what they should have done.

Introduce the similar story that Jesus told, asking for volunteers to come out and be the king and the two servants. Get the children to act out what happens in the story as you go along.

Make the point clearly that Christians believe that God forgives them for wrong things they do and they must be ready to forgive people who hurt them.

Finish with the song 'God loves you and I love you' (*Junior Praise 2*).

Class work

* Use the story of *Miles and the Computer* by Taffy Davies (Scripture Union) as another modern day equivalent of this parable.
* Talk further with the children about how they treat others and how they like to be treated themselves.
* Make up a set of class rules for how to treat others.

13 Frightened friends

Adult led

Aim
To help the children realise that friends may let us down but that Jesus is a friend who will never let us down and will always forgive us.

Bible base
Peter's denial, from John 18 and 21. Peter has declared his faithfulness to Jesus, but Jesus predicts Peter's denial of him. As Jesus is arrested, the other disciples run away, but Peter follows at a distance and waits to see what will happen. In the courtyard of the High Priest's house Peter is challenged by several people as being one of Jesus' followers. Peter is so afraid that he denies three times that he knows Jesus. The cock crows and he realises what he has done.

After his resurrection Jesus speaks particularly to Peter. He asks him three times 'Do you love me?' Each time Peter responds 'Yes, Lord'. Perhaps Peter is asked the question three times to correspond with the three times he denied knowing Jesus. It is obvious that Jesus has forgiven Peter as he commissions him, 'Take care of my sheep'.

Preparation
Collect together: a picture of a fire, three large cards or wooden spoons with 'NO' written on them, some

feathers, some tissues, a fishing net, and three large cards or wooden spoons with 'YES' written on them. Put these in a box to have on your knee and pull out objects at appropriate points.

Presentation

Talk about times when we let our friends down and how we and they feel. Discuss what a good friend should be like and remind the children that none of us are perfect friends.

Explain to the children that Peter was one of Jesus' best friends and had told Jesus he would always stick by him. Then tell the story, drawing out of the box the various items or words. Ask the children to hold them up.

Emphasise Jesus' love and forgiveness for Peter. Three times Peter had said No, that he didn't even know Jesus and as he is reconciled with the risen Jesus three times he says Yes, he loves him and is given a special job by Jesus.

Finish the assembly with a prayer asking for God's help to be good friends who stick by each other.

An appropriate song would be 'One man was Peter' (*Spring Harvest Kids Praise*).

Class work

↓ very sad.

* Make a large class collage of a cockerel. This activity provides an opportunity to discover the different colours of the feathers.
* Discuss fears that the children have and ways in which their friends can help them.
* Look at different types of fish and different methods of fishing.

14 Faithful friends

Adult led

Aim
To help the children appreciate that good friends are those who stick by you and help you even when things get tough.

Bible base
1 Samuel 20. The story of David and Jonathan.

Preparation
Prepare a short, secret message in advance. For example, this could be in a simple code, in white wax crayon ready to paint over, or a message in a bottle written in invisible ink (lemon juice) which is visible when heated by a match. Borrow a child's toy bow and arrow and collect or make the following head dresses to tell the story: cloth and band (David); small crown (Jonathan); large crown (Saul).

Presentation
Talk about secret messages or signals. Display your secret message so that everyone can see it and invite a child to work it out/wash over it to reveal 'A good friend always sticks by you.'

Show the children the bow and arrow and tell them that in the story today you will be telling them how a bow and arrow was used to give a secret signal.

Tell the story from 1 Samuel 20 very simply using volunteers as the three main characters (wearing the head dress) to act as you go along. Explain what the secret signal was and demonstrate the arrow being shot near and far. Then explain what the secret signal meant.

Talk to the children about how Jonathan and David must have felt and how Jonathan helped David even when it was dangerous for him to do so because of Saul's jealousy and anger.

Remind the children that God wants us to be good friends to each other, and talk about different ways we can do this.

Finish the assembly with an appropriate prayer asking that God will help us to be good friends to each other.

Class work
* Look at Morse code, semaphore, and other secret signs.
* Encourage the children to invent their own secret codes.
* Develop work on 'Friends' by designing 'Wanted . . . a friend who is . . .' posters.

15 Forever friends

Adult led

Aim
To help the children discover how Jesus can be a friend.

Bible base
Mark 10 v13–16. Jesus welcomes the children. Matthew 28 v20. Jesus said, 'I will be with you always.'

Preparation
Make, buy or borrow a hand puppet of some kind, an animal or a person to act as your friend. Find some pictures from comics or books of friends who usually go together, eg Pooh and Piglet, Mickey and Minnie Mouse, Bananaman and Spotty, Postman Pat and Jess etc. Mount these and stick one of the 'pair' on a board.

Presentation
Introduce the children to your puppet friend. Tell them about times when your friend has helped you, made you laugh, cheered you up, stuck up for you, etc. Ask the children what they like best about having friends. Then stick up on a board one half of each of the pairs of friends that you have prepared. Go through all the pictures asking the children to guess who their friends are.

Tell the children briefly about the time when children were brought to Jesus (Mark 10 v13–16). Remind them of his promise to be with us always. Talk about how

Christians believe that he is with us today through the Holy Spirit whom we cannot see but who can be with everyone everywhere all the time.

Sing together one or both of the following:

'Jesus, Jesus' (*Spring Harvest Kids Praise*).

'If you climb to the top of a mountain' (*Junior Praise 2*).

Class work

* Look at other stories which show Jesus caring, loving, forgiving, healing, eg feeding the five thousand (Matthew 14 v13–21) where he showed that he cared that the people were hungry; washing the disciples feet (John 13 v1–17) where Jesus showed love to his disciples; Peter's denial (Luke 22 v54–62) and where Jesus showed that he had forgiven Peter (John 21 v15–17).

* Prepare two pictures of a child's face, one looking miserable, the other smiling. Each should have a slit at the top in which the different characteristics will be placed. Look at different qualities, eg sharing, being jealous, arguing, helping. Decide whether each quality is a good thing or bad thing to have in friendships and add it to the appropriate head, eg sharing to the smiley one, being jealous to the miserable one.

16 Which friend are you like?

Adult led

Aim
To help the children think about how they behave and treat their friends.

Preparation
Draw pictures of four children, three looking grumpy, selfish and sulky and one looking cheerful. Alternatively you could use puppets or paint faces on eggs.

Presentation
Explain to the children that you are going to show them four friends from school. Are they like any of them?

Gertie Grumble
Gertie grumbles about all sorts of things. When she's at home she grumbles about getting up because she likes to sleep in. She grumbles about tidying up her room; she'd rather watch television. When she goes shopping to the supermarket she moans all the way round; it's far too boring. She grumbles about going to school, especially having to walk. She grumbles about doing any writing or reading; she'd rather play in the home-corner. She grumbles at playtime because people won't play her games.

Willy Won't
When he gets up Willy won't eat breakfast, he always wants a different cereal. On the way to school Willy

won't hurry, no matter how much his mum tries, so he's often late. Willy won't finish his work on time. When the teacher asks the children to pack up, Willy doesn't; he carries on for another five minutes. At playtime when the other children are playing with a ball Willy won't be sensible. At home Willy refuses to put away his reading book; he leaves it on the floor in the hall. At bedtime he won't go to bed without a fuss.

Sally Selfish

When Sally is at school she never wants to share the crayons, plasticine or sand toys. At playtime she won't let anyone else use her skipping rope until she's bored with it. If the teacher asks the children to sit on the carpet, Sally makes sure she is always at the front and she calls out all the answers. When the class lines up for PE, Sally pushes to the front of the line. On arriving home Sally runs for the biscuit tin and eats all the chocolate biscuits before her brother gets home. She won't even share her toys with her little sister.

Charlie Cheerful

When Charlie arrives at school he waves goodbye to his mum and gives his teacher a big smile. He gets on with his work straight away. He is always happy to help his teacher with even the most boring of jobs. At playtime he often has lots of friends to play with and he makes sure no one is left out. At home Charlie tries to remember to make his bed every day. He and his sister take it in turns to do errands for their mum. He likes to visit his grandma who is poorly. He often makes her a cup of tea to cheer her up.

Class work

* Finish the sentence 'A good friend is . . .'
* Make a code of friendship to display in the classroom.
* Make a word-box containing words about friendship.

17 Friendship cake

Adult led

Aim
To show the children that the little we have to offer can be used by God and is of value to him.

Bible base
Matthew 13 v33. The Parable of the Yeast. Jesus uses the picture of yeast causing dough to rise to explain the spread of God's kingdom from inconspicuous beginnings.

Preparation
Props: three bowls (small, medium and large); a jar of yeast mixture; a tea-towel. You might like to make a cake for the children to taste.

This assembly is based on the idea of friendship cakes where some cake mixture is passed on to other people to 'multiply' the cake. The process is spread over ten days, during which time the yeast is feeding on the sugar.

Presentation
Show the children a jar with some yeast mixture. Ask a volunteer to come and smell it to see if they can guess what it is. Tell the children that this is the beginning of a cake. Have they heard about friendship cakes? This is the story of what happened when you tried to make a friendship cake.

Act out the following story, but do not use real ingredients.

On day one I put 1 cup of flour, 1 cup of sugar and 1 cup of milk plus the yeast mixture in to a bowl and stirred. (*Use the smallest bowl first.*) I left the mixture and went shopping.

On day two I stirred the mixture again. When I looked into the bowl the mixture had started to bubble. I left it and went and did the gardening.

On day three I did not check it but got on with other things.

On day four I took a look. To my amazement the tea-towel which had been lying over the bowl had been pulled downwards and the mixture was climbing over the edge of the bowl. I transferred everything into a slightly larger bowl.

On day five I added more cups of flour, sugar and milk plus some more yeast mixture and then went about my business.

On day six I stirred it really well and got some of my family to have a stir as well.

On day seven it was bubbling along and making all sorts of noises.

On day eight I checked the bowl again. The tea-towel had been pulled down *again* and the mixture was escaping from the bowl. I was worried that I might end up with a huge slime monster in my kitchen! I transferred the mixture into a bigger bowl.

On day nine I was busy and forgot to check the mixture.

On day ten I stirred it well and removed three cups of the mixture to give to three friends. I added the other ingredients, eggs, plus other things like sultanas, mixed spice, apples etc to the mixture that was left and then baked it in the oven. (*Ask for some volunteers to try the cake*).

Compare the size of the jar and the large bowl and

comment on how the little bit in the jar grew to fill a huge bowl. What causes this? Yeast. Jesus talked about yeast making dough rise. Just like the yeast can make a big difference, what you do is valuable to God and he can use it to make a big difference.

Class work
* Talk about things we can do that make a big difference, eg being cheerful when we clear up, smiling at people in our class, trying hard with our work.
* Look at the assembly 'Hungry and Full' for other ideas.

Colour and light

18 God was pleased

Class led

Aim
To teach the children that the Bible says that God made the world and that he also made us.

Bible base
Genesis 1.

Preparation
Class-led assembly. Make a collection with the class of 'natural' objects, eg fruit, shells, flowers, etc, or pictures of beautiful landscapes or animals. Discuss which of these are the children's favourite ones and why. Hide these 'favourites' in a large bag.

Ask members of the class to bring in old T-shirts to decorate. Get hold of some fabric paints suitable for the children to use.

Learn together as a class 'Creation Song' from *Ishmael's Family Worship Book*.

Explain to the children that the T-shirts will illustrate what God made on each of the six days. For example Day 4's T-shirt will show sun, moon, stars. Let the children create a design and work on the T-shirts in groups (alternatively, use six fairly large sheets of strong card to paint on). There should be one T-shirt/picture for each day. Day 1 – light, Day 2 – sea and sky, Day 3 –

land, plant, seeds, Day 4 – sun, moon, stars, Day 5 –
fish and birds, Day 6 – animals and humans. Encourage
a few of the children to write their own thank-you prayers for creation.

Presentation

Welcome the children to assembly and ask for a volunteer to come and choose an object from the 'mystery' bag
explaining that the class has been discussing some of
the beautiful things we can see in our world.

As the various objects/pictures are pulled from the bag
hold them up for everyone to see and ask a member of
the class to say why it was a particular favourite.

Perhaps using a large children's picture Bible, explain
to the children that the very first story tells us about
the time when Christians believe God made the world
and all the beautiful things in it. Then invite children
from the class to come out and put on the T-shirts or
hold up the pictures while the rest of the class sing
'Creation Song'. Talk particularly about Day 1 when God
made light and Day 4 when God made the sun, the
moon, and the stars. What would happen if there were
no sun? Can they name any of the stars?

Finish the assembly with thank-you prayers for what
God has made, read by members of the class.

Another appropriate song for all to sing is 'There are
hundreds of sparrows' (*Junior Praise 1*).

Class work

* Do some experiments using light. For example, grow
some seeds with light and some without.
* Talk about shadows and make some shadow puppets.
Make a sun-dial.
* Look at some of the star shapes and names.
* Read and discuss other creation stories from other
faiths, if appropriate.

19 Mr Noah

Adult led

Aim
To help the children understand that God never breaks his promises.

Bible base
Genesis 6 v9 – 9 v17.

Preparation
Collect a few props for the volunteers who will help you tell the story, eg hats, letter, toy tools, book on caring for animals, spade, hay, oats, umbrellas, waterproofs, sunglasses and a rainbow (this can be made from thin strips of coloured crepe paper joined together and rolled up.)

Presentation
Tell the children that today they will hear a story that they have probably heard before but that this time it will be told in a special way. Ask for five volunteers to be Mr Noah, Mrs Noah, Ham, Shem and Japheth.

Narrate the following sketch and hand out the relevant props as you go along.

There was a man called Noah.

He had three fine sons. Their names were Ham, Shem, and Japheth.

Noah also had a wife. The Bible doesn't tell us her name, so for now let's call her Hilda!

When Noah was alive the world was young and beautiful. You might almost say it was freshly baked as God had only just made it. Everything was all right in the world except the people. Wherever God looked he saw people arguing, destroying the beauty of his earth, killing each other, fighting with each other, hurting each other.

God was angry and hurt at the way they were behaving, but they did not care about God any more, so they didn't take much notice.

God decided that something needed to be done. He decided on a giant clean-up operation. He did not forget that some people might be hurt, so he decided to let people know what was going on.

He looked over the whole earth but could find only Noah who loved him enough to listen to him. The Bible does not say how God told Noah about the flood. Let's imagine that he wrote a letter to him.

Noah was certainly not expecting a letter from God when suddenly there it was, delivered by Red Star, a message from God. He read it carefully:

Dear Noah,
Sorry to bother you, but this is an emergency. The earth is in a dreadful state. I can't bear it any longer so I'm going to clean it up. There will be a big flood on.... at about... (add the day and time of the assembly). *Be prepared. Build an ark (you will find a detailed plan in the envelope). Take into it people who don't think you're silly and will help you. Take two of all the animals you can find.*
Don't forget your wife!
Love from God.

Noah was surprised but because he loved God, he trusted him. He gathered everything ready, he gathered his sons, he even gathered his wife and they began to build.

Every morning you would see Noah and at least one of his sons working – sawing wood, lifting huge planks, hammering nails. Even Hilda helped grumpily.

Many of Noah's friends came to see the strange sight of Mr Noah building something out of wood in his back garden. Even though he felt silly, Noah was sure that God would not let him down.

Eventually as day approached God told Noah to gather the animals for the ark. Soon, from all directions you could see animals, running steadily towards the ark.

Mr Noah sorted them out. He gave the fierce animals strict instructions not to harm any other animal while they were on the ark. The animals agreed and Noah packed them in as tightly and neatly as possible, which wasn't easy with so many of them. When all the animals and Noah's family were inside, God closed the door.

The rain started to pour down from the sky. The waters began to rise, the wind to howl. This made the animals restless, you can imagine the dreadful noise when they all started to yowl together.

The ark was soon floating above everything – towns, woods, hills – nothing could be seen, but still the rain continued.

Mr Noah and his family settled down to life on board the ark, but they soon grew very bored.

Then one day there was no rain. After a while Mr Noah began to wonder if any dry land had appeared. He made up a plan to find out. He would send out a bird to see if it could land anywhere.

The first bird, a raven, flew around for a while but did not find anywhere to land so it came back.

The second bird, a dove, fluttered above their heads and then set off for the east. She came back with a twig and leaves in her beak.

Mr Noah and his family were very excited. This meant land had appeared. Some days later Noah sent out the dove again. It circled the ark and flew off towards the east where a few glimmers of sunshine were appearing. They never saw it again. This meant there was dry land at last and the end of the flood.

A few days later Mr Noah and his family woke up to see a huge warm sun rising. They all took huge mouthfuls of the lovely fresh air.

Then they noticed that the ark had come to rest. Noah and his family and the animals, clambered out onto the land and looked about them.

God wanted to send a kind of 'Welcome Home' card and also to promise them that there would be no more giant clean-up operations like that one. So he gathered together his seven favourite colours and flung them in a beautiful arc across the sky. Then he called down to Noah, his family and the animals. 'Be at peace. Live happily, have many children and fill the earth again. Whenever you see a rainbow remember, I promise never to flood the earth again and I can be trusted.'

Ask the children why God decided to send the flood, and ask them why Noah and his family were safe.

Remind them that there has never been another flood over the whole earth and talk about what the rainbow stands for.

Finish by singing 'Mister Noah built an ark' (*Junior Praise 1*) or 'Who built the ark?' (*Someone's singing Lord*).

20 Follow that star

Adult led

Aim
To look at how God used a star to guide the wise men to Jesus and how following Jesus, the light of the world, can help us.

(The assembly 'Light and dark' has further suggestions on this theme.)

Bible base
Matthew 2 v1–12, John 8 v12.

Preparation
Collect together different types of lights – torch, candle, light bulb, headlamp, picture of lighthouse, etc.

Have two connecting wires, a battery and a bulb. Make a fairly large card star and decorate it with glitter, shiny paper etc. Suspend it on a thread attached to a stick.

Presentation
Ask a child to come out and get the bulb to light up using the batteries and connecting wires. Discuss how and when lights help us and a little of how they work. They can guide us so we go the right way. It would be very hard without them. Produce your shiny star dangling from a stick.

Ask the children if they know a story from the Bible which tells when God used a star to help to guide some people. Choose a child to walk in front holding the star up and some children to follow representing the wise men. They could walk once round the hall/room. Then ask where the star guided the wise men to first and choose a child to be Herod. Fill in what happens at the palace and how the star appears again to guide them to baby Jesus.

Choose a Mary and Joseph and have the wise men walk over to them following the star. Get all the volunteers to sit down and discuss how God had sent the star to help the wise men find Jesus.

Remind the children that Jesus grew up to be a man and how he said that he was the Light of the World. Christians believe that if people follow Jesus, the Light of the World, he will help them to go the right way in their lives.

Say a prayer thanking Jesus that he is like a light to guide us.

Class work
Read the picture book *'Casper and the star'* by Francesca Bosca (Lion Publishing).

About me

21 Feelings

Adult led

Aim
To help the children understand that God knows and cares about how we are feeling.

Bible base
Psalm 139 v1–5.

Preparation
Draw faces on paper plates, showing different emotions, eg happy, sad, angry, worried.

Presentation
Hold up the faces one at a time and ask the children 'What's this person feeling like? What sorts of things make you feel ... (happy, sad, etc)?' Talk about how sometimes what you feel is shown by your expression,

but sometimes nobody else knows what you're feeling inside.

Christians believe that even when nobody else knows, God knows what you are feeling. In the Bible there is a poem by a man called David telling God what he thinks about that:

Lord, you have examined me and you know me.
You know everything I do;
From far away you understand all my thoughts.
You see me whether I am working or resting;
You know all my actions.
Even before I speak you already know what I will say.
You are all around me on every side;
You protect me with your power.

Finish the assembly by singing 'My Lord is Higher than a Mountain' (*Junior Praise 1*).

Class work

* Let the children make up 'My Happy Day' and 'A Very Sad Day' stories.
* Discuss together how certain words make them feel, eg drizzle, shouting, presents, dark, etc and make up a class book of happy and sad words.
* Look at the assembly *Tears and Smiles*.

22 Shoes

Adult led

Aim
To show we're all special to God.

Bible base
There are many verses which show we are special to God, eg Zephaniah 3 v17, Isaiah 43 v1–4, Romans 8 v28, Ephesians 2 v10.

Preparation

Collect together different types of shoes, eg a Wellington boot, slipper, walking boot, running shoe, flip flop, 'smart' shoe.

Presentation
Show the children the different types of shoes. With each item of footwear ask the children when you would wear them, eg splashing in puddles, in the house, going on long walks, playing tennis, on the beach, going to a wedding! Then ask them which shoe they think that you like best, and gives reasons why, eg the running shoe because you play a lot of tennis.

Explain that actually you like all the shoes the same. They are all special to you because they are different and you can wear them on different occasions. It would look silly if you wore your slippers on the beach, or your wellingtons playing tennis, or your walking boots with your pyjamas etc.

Go on to say that we are all like the shoes in a way. Just as all the shoes are important to you, each of us is special to God. The Bible says that he made each one of us differently and each of us has things that we are particularly good at. It could be drawing, writing, helping tidy up etc but it doesn't matter which, we are *all* special to God.

Class work

* Read 'Napoleon the Envious Earwig' from the book *Ignatius Goes Fishing* by Philip Welsh, (Scripture Union).

* Pass round a 'magic box' with a mirror inside it. Explain to the children there is something very special inside it. Tell them to have a look, but don't tell anyone what they see.

* Each child brings in a photo of themselves, sticks the photo on a piece of paper and then writes or draws around the photo under the headings 'My special people', 'My special places', 'What I'm good at', to show that each of them is unique.

23 The tool box

Adult led

Aim
To show that we are all special to God.

This assembly is on the same theme as the one called *Shoes*.

Preparation
Props needed: a tool-box with various tools inside.

Presentation
Bring in a tool-box and explain to the children what all the various tools are used for. Then tell them the following story, adapting it according to the tools you have available!

All was not well in the workshop belonging to Mr Teak the carpenter. There was a lot of noise and arguing going on. All the different tools were trying to decide which of them was the best.

The hammer said, 'I must be the best. Think of all the power I have. No nail is too big for me.'

'Ah, that sums you up,' said the set square, 'all muscle and no brains. My work takes skill, measuring angles and so on.'

'You're such a square! Ha, ha. Now *I* have things taped!' Can you guess which one is speaking now? Yes, the tape measure!

And so it went on, each of the tools in the shed had their say . . . the screwdriver, the spirit level. (*Go through each of the tools presenting their argument. Then ask the children to vote for which one they think is the best.*)

At this point the carpenter, Mr Teak, came into the shed to find out what all the noise was. He quickly discovered what they were all arguing about. They asked him which tool he thought was the best. He thought for a while. Then he said, 'You all realise that you each have a special job to do. However, none of you is more important than any of the others. When I am making a table I need all of you. Having just one of you would be hopeless. Besides which, have you ever thought that actually you are *all* useless until picked up and used by me?'

Draw a parallel with each of us having special gifts and that actually we work best when we ask God to help us.

Class work
See the ideas from the *Shoes* assembly.

24 Whom can I help?

Adult and class led

Aim
To think about people who need help and how we can help them.

Bible base
Luke 10 v25–37. The Parable of the Good Samaritan. This story is about a traveller who is beaten up by robbers and left for dead. The priest and the Levite were important respected people, and they thought they were doing right, but it was the Samaritan who proved himself to be the true neighbour, or friend.

This is a good story for the children to try and explore each of the characters and their part in the story.

The traveller – rather foolish: people usually travelled on the Jerusalem to Jericho road with others, particularly if they were carrying valuables.

The priest – to touch a dead man would make him unclean for seven days and prevent him from doing his work at the Temple.

The Levite – sometimes bandits used a wounded person as a decoy and then attacked someone who stopped to help. The Levite was worried for his own safety.

The Samaritan – traditionally the Jews and the Samaritans were enemies. He overcame his hostility to show compassion to someone in need.

Preparation

The children could make puppets to retell the story. One idea is to use plastic milk containers; the handles make very good noses! Add wool for hair, felt for eyes etc. A rug or sheet can form the puppet theatre. Practise the play. The teacher or a child narrates the story whilst some children move the puppets.

Presentation

Narrator: One day, Jesus told the people, 'You must love God with all your heart and love other people as much as you love yourself.'

'We don't understand. What do you mean?' the people asked. So Jesus told them this story.

A man was making his way down a road from Jerusalem to Jericho. It was a lonely road.
(*Puppet walks along the road, looking left and right.*)

Suddenly robbers jumped out from behind some bushes. They threw him to the ground, beat him up and stole his money and clothes.
(*Other puppets jump up and attack the first one.*)

The poor man lay by the roadside. He was almost dead. The first person to come along was a priest. He did not stop because he did not want to touch the man.
(*Priest puppet pauses, looks but hurries past.*)

Before too long another man came past. He worked at the temple. He did not stop either, he was afraid he might get attacked by the robbers too.
(*Levite puppet crosses the road and hurries by.*)

'Help me, someone!' the man called.

The next man who came by was a Samaritan. He was a long way from home. I wonder if he helped? (*Here the puppet nods his head.*) Yes, for when he saw the man he felt sorry for him. He cleaned up his cuts and put ointment on them and bandaged the man up. Then the Samaritan carefully put the man on his donkey and slowly they travelled to an inn.

'Please give this man some food and a good bed,' the Samaritan said to the innkeeper. He also handed over some money. 'If this is not enough, I shall give you more when I return,' he said.

Jesus asked, 'Which one showed the most kindness?' (*Here the three passer-by puppets can reappear.*)
(*The children can be given the opportunity to reply.*)

Jesus then said, 'You should help other people as the Samaritan did.'

Class work

* Make a frieze of the characters in the story. Ask the children what they might have been thinking and then show these ideas in thought bubbles.
* Talk about times when the children need help. Who helps them? What if their mum, dad, teacher, or friend did not? Who can the children help and how? Is there anyone they would not help? Should they?
* Draw a child's face and then tell a story about her day: She is slow getting up and her mum calls her lazy; she trips up on the way into the playground and everyone laughs; her teacher gets cross with her because she forgot her reading book; someone calls her names, etc.

After each incident ask one of the children to come and rip off a piece of her face to give a visual representation of how she feels. Talk about how the children think they might be able to help her.

Role-play simple situations in pairs when someone has been horrible to their partner. What could they say?
* Explain that Christians say Jesus teaches them to help anyone who needs help. Look briefly at the work of the Children's Society, TEAR Fund, Christian Aid to show this in practice.
* Read *Wayne Hoskins and the Pram Lady*, a retelling of this story, by Jennifer Gubb, (Meridor books).
* Other resources: *Lion Children's Bible Series no. 38, The Good Samaritan* (Palm Tree).

25 Our special things

Adult and class led

Aim
To show that God is a bit like treasure, he is so special.

Bible base
Matthew 13 v44–46. Hidden treasure/Precious pearl. These two short parables are used by Jesus to express the excitement of discovering God and his kingdom. For Christians the experience of God's love and the challenge it brings are of inestimable worth.

Preparation
Ask the children what is their most precious 'thing'? Would they swap it for anything else? If so, what?

Ask the children to paint their favourite thing or bring it in to school.

Tell the children the stories of the hidden treasure and the precious pearl. The stories are told well in *The precious pearl* by Butterworth and Inkpen (Marshall Pickering) and *Hidden Treasure* by Jeffs and Hicks (Bible Society).

Role-play the two men making their discoveries. How would they have felt? What would the children have done?

Presentation
Show the children things which are very precious to you. The children in your class could show some of their

valuable things or the pictures they have painted.

Tell the two stories while a couple of children mime the actions. The following is a brief outline for the hidden treasure. Add more detail as appropriate.

It was a sunny day and Bert decided he would go on a picnic. He packed up some of his favourite sandwiches, banana and honey, and off he set. Before long he found a little field. Bert decided this would be a good spot. He climbed over the stile and settled down for lunch.

Now Bert had brought along his metal detector. Looking for old bits of metal was one of his favourite hobbies. After a while there was a buzzing noise. Bert stopped the machine and began to dig. Imagine his delight when he found an old wooden box. Inside there were beautiful jewels and gold coins.

Bert buried his discovery and rushed home. Excitedly he told the news to his wife, Ethel. Ethel and Bert went to the estate agents and found that the field was for sale. They decided to sell their house, their furniture and even their clothes so that they could buy the field.

The children could also show their role-plays here.

Explain that Christians think that God is a bit like treasure, because he is so special.

Class work
* Talk about finding special things, opening surprise presents, deciding what things are worth.
* Make a collage of a treasure chest and write the story up next to it or in the lid of the chest.
* Each child could bring in a photo of themselves, stick the photo on a piece of paper and then write around the photo under the headings 'My special things', 'My special places', 'My special people'.
* Ask different children to bring in something that is special to them, to talk to their class about it and to answer questions their friends ask about it.
* Have a treasure hunt.

26 Appearances

Adult led

Aim
To show that God cares about what we are like inside, not what we look like on the outside.

Bible base
1 Samuel 16 v1–13. David is chosen to be king. Saul, the present king, has been disobeying God and God rejects him as king. God sends Samuel, his prophet, to choose a new king from the family of Jesse. Samuel is not to focus on the outward features, which had characterised Saul. God is concerned about people's inner character.

Preparation
Prepare three parcels. Wrap a stone and also a potato in pretty wrapping paper, and wrap a bag of sweets in newspaper.

Presentation
Ask three children to come and choose a parcel. Usually the 'pretty' parcels are chosen first (unless they have done this before!). Explain that we can't always tell what something is like on the inside just by looking at them.

People can be like that. You cannot tell if someone is nice just by looking at them. You have to get to know them to find out what they are like on the 'inside'.

This story shows that God is more interested in what we are like on the inside. It's a story about choosing a king a long time ago in a country called Israel, many, many miles away.

The man whose job it was to go and choose people to be king was called Samuel. He was an old man, who went everywhere leaning on a stick. But although he was old, he was very wise, and more than that, he was special. Samuel was special because he had been chosen to do a special job by God, to go round choosing kings, and then to help the kings to do the right things. God does not always choose young, strong people to do his work. He just wants the right people at the right time, whether they are old or young.

One day God told Samuel to go to a little village called Bethlehem. It was the village where a man called Jesse and his family lived. God told Samuel, 'I want you to go and choose someone to be king.'

So Samuel did as he was told. He packed his bags, taking care to take his 'king-making kit', which was a little bottle of oil. When Samuel had chosen the right person to be king, he would pour a little of the oil over his head.

When Samuel reached Bethlehem, he went straight to Jesse's house, and he said to Jesse, 'Call your sons in from the fields. I have something very important to say to you all. Meet me for a special lunch at the village hall.'

So Jesse, wondering what was up, called all his sons in from the fields, except for one. He didn't bother with David because he was the youngest and the smallest. Jesse thought that nothing Samuel would say would interest David, and anyway, someone had to look after the sheep.

When Jesse and his sons reached the village hall they found the tables spread for a wonderful meal. But before they could sit down Samuel asked them to come and stand near him. Samuel said, 'Jesse, please ask your sons to stand in a line. God has asked me to choose a new king, and he has told me it is to be one of your sons.' So the seven sons who were there with their father Jesse went and stood in a line. (*Ask for seven children to come out and stand in a line as Jesse's sons.*)

Samuel looked along the line. 'Which one would I choose for king? They all look so good.' All the sons looked strong and tough and wise.

Samuel looked first at Eliab. 'Just look at his strong arms,' thought Samuel, but then he heard God say, 'No, not that one.'

So then Samuel looked at Abinadab. 'Just look at his strong legs,' thought Samuel, but then he heard God say, 'No, not that one.'

Then Samuel looked at Shammah. 'Just look at his wise eyes,' but then he heard God say, 'No, not that one.'

Then Samuel looked at son number 4. 'Just look at his powerful feet,' but then he heard God say 'No, not that one.'

Then Samuel looked at son number 5. 'Just look at his strong mouth,' but then he heard God say, 'No, not that one.'

Then Samuel looked at son number 6. 'Just look at his beautiful head,' but then he heard God say, 'No, not that one.'

By now there was only one son left standing in the line. Samuel thought, 'This must be the one. Just look at his broad chest,' but then he heard God say, 'No, not that one.'

By now, Samuel was getting quite upset as he had run out of sons to choose. He said to God, 'Well, if you don't mind me saying so, they looked all right to me.'

'Ah well, Samuel,' said God, 'you are only looking at the outside, but I can see what a person is like on the inside. I can see whether a person is honest, I can see if a person is caring, I can see if a person is brave . . . You cannot see those things, Samuel, but I can. Everyone is special to me and it is what is on the inside that counts. Ask Jesse if he has any more sons.'

So Samuel did, and Jesse said, 'Well, there is David, but he's the youngest and the smallest. He is out looking after the sheep, but I will call him if you like.'

'Please do', said Samuel. So Jesse sent Eliab to go and get David. (*Send the child chosen as Eliab to go and get a David from the group.*) David came into the Village Hall, full of life. He had run all the way so his face was quite red, and his hair stuck up because of the wind. 'Boy, you are young,' said Samuel. But God said, 'Yes, he's the one I want you to choose for king. David is the one.'

You see, when God chooses people, he does not always pick the strongest and the biggest. He picks the right person for the job, after he has looked at their thoughts. We are all special to God, and he has something special for all of us to do.

Samuel now got out his king-making kit. He was going to put some oil on David's forehead so that his family would know that God had chosen him to be king.

Class work
* Read 'It's not much fun being a slug' from *Ignatius goes fishing* by Philip Welsh, (Scripture Union).
* Give to the children a number of qualities, eg kindness, sense of humour, lots of toys, good-looks and ask them which are important when they are choosing a friend.
* Look at the assembly *Little and Large* for another story in David's life.

27 Things that worry us

Adult led

Aim
To look at the things that worry us and to show that God cares.

Bible base
Matthew 6 v25–34. God's care of the birds and flowers.

This passage is part of Jesus' famous teaching, the Sermon on the Mount. Jesus teaches that God does not want us to spend all our time worrying about practical details. God knows and cares about our needs.

Preparation
Draw a picture of a child looking worried. Write out each word of the verse 1 Peter 5 v7 (Good News Bible) on a drawing of a sparrow.

Presentation
Show the children a picture of a child called Wendy, looking 'worried'. Ask the children for suggestions as to how she is feeling and also why she might be worried, eg she is worried about forgetting her reading book, no-one to play with etc.

Jesus talks about worrying. He says that we should not spend all our time worrying about things we cannot do anything about, for instance what is going to happen tomorrow. He says that if you look at the birds in the sky they do not worry and God takes care of them. If God looks after flowers in the field how much more will he look after people. For we are all much more precious to God than the birds or the flowers.

Tell the children about the verse 1 Peter 5 v7 'Leave all your worries with God, because he cares for you' (Good News Bible). Show the words written out on the sparrow. The Bible says that God understands when we are worried.

Learn and sing the song 'Sometimes problems can be big' (*Children's Praise*).

Class work
* Read *The Very Worried Sparrow* by Meryl Doney (Lion) and *Where the wild things are* by Maurice Sendak (Picture Puffin).
* In a circle each child says 'I feel worried/frightened when . . .'
* Write some worries/fears, eg being in my room in the dark. Put them in a hat, pull them out and ask for suggestions about what might help.

28 Daniel and the lions

Adult led

Aim
To explore the idea of doing what you know is right.

Bible base
Daniel 6. Daniel and the lions.

   Daniel was a Jew who had been taken into exile in Babylon. By his wisdom he had become an important man in the kingdom, so many of the native rulers were jealous of him. They plotted to get rid of him. They were unable to find anything that Daniel did wrong so they 'framed' him. Because he stood up for what he believed in, he got into trouble, but God was able to rescue him.

Preparation
No props needed. During the story the children could be asked to perform certain actions on key words. For example when 'the king' is mentioned the children could bow their heads, when 'Daniel' is heard they could pretend to pray and when 'lions' are mentioned they can roar.

Presentation
Have the children ever found it difficult to do what they know is right? It can be hard, especially if your friends or other people do not want you to. Listen to what hap-

pened to a man who stood up for what he knew was right, even though it would get him into trouble.

Tell the story from Daniel 6 or use the following outline.

Every morning when Daniel woke up, he knelt by the window of his room and prayed. He told God how unhappy he was that he couldn't live in his own land. He asked God to help him in this strange land where he had to work now.

Every afternoon, when it was too hot to work, Daniel knelt by the window of his room. He talked to God about what he'd done in the morning. He asked God to make him a good worker.

Every night, before going to sleep, Daniel knelt by the window of his room. He thanked God that King Darius was his friend. He asked God to help him serve the king well.

King Darius liked Daniel because he was clever. He helped the king rule the land, but other men hated Daniel.

'The king only listens to Daniel now,' they grumbled. 'He never listens to us.'

'Let's watch Daniel carefully,' one man said. 'When he does something wrong, we will tell King Darius.'

'Yes,' said another. 'Then the king will be angry with Daniel and send him away.'

So, these unkind men began to watch all Daniel did. They saw how hard he worked, but he never did anything wrong, not once. They also saw that he knelt by his window three times a day – every morning when he woke up, every afternoon when it was too hot to work and every night before going to sleep.

'It's no good,' the men said to each other. 'We'll never get rid of Daniel like this. We must think of another way.'

Soon they had thought of a cruel trick to trap Daniel.

The men went to the king. 'Your Majesty,' they said,

bowing, 'you are a great king. Now, why don't you make a law which everyone must obey. Tell all the people that, if they want anything at all, they must ask you for it. They must not ask their friends or neighbours. They must not even ask their families for help. They must ask only you.'

King Darius was pleased. 'That will make everyone understand what a great and good king I am,' he agreed.

The men smiled. 'And if anyone does not obey the law, your Majesty, you should put them in a pit with your lions.'

'Yes,' said the king. 'I will do that.'

He was so pleased with the new law that he didn't think what might happen. Later he was sorry.

In a few days the men came back.

'Your Majesty,' they said, 'You remember your new law? You ordered the people to ask for help only from you.'

Of course the king remembered! He was very pleased about it.

'Well,' they said, 'someone is not obeying your law.'

The king was angry. 'Then he must be thrown into the lions' pit!' he shouted. 'Let the lions eat him for not obeying me! Who is it?'

'It is Daniel,' the men said. 'Every morning when he wakes up he kneels by his window and asks God to help him. Every afternoon when it's too hot to work he does the same. And every night before he goes to sleep he prays again. Daniel is breaking your law.'

Now the king was quiet. Daniel was his friend. He didn't want him to die.

'You can't change the law,' the men told him. 'You must do what you said.'

King Darius knew he had made a mistake. He tried to find a way of saving Daniel, but at last he had to agree to have him thrown into the lions' pit.

He was very upset. The lions roared fiercely as Daniel

was taken to the pit.

'But your God might save you!' King Darius called after him, though he didn't really believe he'd see Daniel again.

All that night he thought about Daniel. He was so worried that he couldn't eat or sleep. As soon as it was light enough to see, he ran to the deep pit where the lions were kept.

He called, 'Daniel!', wondering whether his friend would answer or whether there would be silence.

How happy he was when he heard Daniel answer, 'Your Majesty, I am here. The lions have not hurt me.'

King Darius ran forward and ordered his servants to pull Daniel out. Soon his friend was back with him. 'I did nothing wrong,' Daniel told him, 'and God kept me safe.'

'Your God is great!' cried the overjoyed king. 'Everyone should pray to him, Daniel, just as you do.'

Everyone thought Daniel would die but God looked after him.

Class work

* Discuss with the children what kind of decisions they make and who influences those decisions.
* Talk with the children about times when the children have had to do things which they know are right, but it was hard, eg owning up to breaking something.
* Give the children simple case studies about stealing, lying etc and ask them what they would do. Role-play some of these situations where the children have to make a choice about doing the 'right' thing.
* Talk about other situations when they have needed to be brave. What things are they particularly scared of?
* Let the children imagine that they are either the king or Daniel. What would they have been thinking during the night when he was in the lions' den?

29 Thunderbirds – International Rescue

Adult and class led (probably year 2)

Aim
To show that God has a plan for our lives.

Bible base
Exodus 2 v1–10. Moses in the bulrushes.

The Pharaoh was feeling threatened by the growing numbers of Israelites. By killing all their baby boys he hoped to reduce the Israelites' potential power. Moses, however, was protected in a special way; he was saved for a purpose.

Preparation
Find various items on the Thunderbird theme, eg hat, comic, theme music. Practise the play. The teacher could narrate while the children act.

Presentation
Play the 'Thunderbirds' theme music and ask the children if they recognise it. Show a Thunderbirds comic/ hat etc and talk about the things that the Thunderbirds do, eg International Rescue.

Tell the story of the dramatic rescue of Moses from the reeds.

Narrator: Egypt was a strong and powerful land. There were many Israelites living in Egypt and the King of Egypt was very angry with all the Israelites. There were too many of them! Day by day the king watched the number of Israelites grow bigger and bigger until he could stand it no more. In a terrible rage he called all his soldiers together and cried out:

Pharaoh: I want you to kill all the baby boys who are born to the Israelites. Get rid of them! Throw them into the river Nile! That will show them how much I hate them.

Narrator: The king had given his orders and his soldiers had to carry them out. As the babies were killed the Israelites wept helplessly and were very sad.

There was one couple among the Israelites who loved and worshipped God. They already had two children, called Miriam and Aaron, and they had just had a little baby boy when the king made his terrible order.

Jochebed: I can't let them take my baby away. He's precious to me and I want to keep him.

Narrator: The baby's mother had a clever idea and called her daughter.

Jochebed: Miriam! Go down to the river and cut some reeds that grow there. Get a big armful. I have a plan to save my baby.

Narrator: When Miriam returned her mother began to work. She made a basket just big enough for the baby to lie in. She made a lid to cover the basket and painted it with a sticky tar.

Jochebed: Now we can hide him in the reeds by the river.

Miriam: I'll watch over him to check that no harm comes to him.

Narrator: Jochebed carefully took the basket down to the river and laid it among the reeds there.

Miriam stayed close by to watch over it. Before long she heard talking and laughing. She peeped out and saw some girls coming down to the river to bathe. One of them was a princess, the king of Egypt's daughter. Suddenly the baby in the basket started to cry. Miriam held her breath as the princess called out to her maids.

Princess: Can you hear that noise? It sounds like a small baby crying. Come and help me look.

Maid: Yes, here it is, a little boy! Isn't he lovely!

Princess: I think he's an Israelite baby. Poor little thing, we can't let him be killed. I'd like to have him for my own, but he's still very small and needs milk.

Narrator: Miriam saw her chance and ran up to the princess.

Miriam: Would you like me to get a nurse to help you look after him?

Princess: Yes, if you know of someone good.

Narrator: Miriam ran home as fast as she could, bursting with excitement.

Miriam: Mother, Mother, come quickly! The princess has found our baby and wants someone to look after him!

Narrator: So Miriam took Jochebed to meet the princess.

Princess: Would you take good care of this little boy that I've found? When he is old enough you may bring him to the palace and I will adopt him as my son. His name shall be Moses because it means I lifted him out of the water.

Jochebed: Of course, your Highness, I'll look after him well. Thank you very much!

Narrator: When they got home with Moses, Miriam and her mother laughed for joy. The whole family cared well for Moses until he was old enough to be taken to the palace. During all this time God took good care of him because he had special plans for Moses' future.

Comment that just as God had a special plan for Moses' life the Bible tells us that he has special plans for each of us.

Class work
* Find out what Moses goes on to do, particularly leading the people out of Egypt across the Red Sea (Exodus 14).
* Talk about any plans that they make, eg for parties.

30 Kangaroos

Adult led

Aim
To show that God loves us and wants to protect us.

Bible base
Proverbs 18 v10. God is like a strong tower – when you run to him, he will keep you safe.

Preparation
Get together a kangaroo poster or picture, a soft toy joey and a tin of baked beans.

Presentation
Show the poster and talk generally about kangaroos. Describe the birth of a roo using a baked bean to show the size of a newborn baby. Explain that the roo carries on feeding and growing in its mother's pouch. In the pouch they have an easy journey, food and safety. Describe how they often run in headfirst! Even when they are quite large, they know they can always run to mum.

The Bible says that God is like that. He is like a strong tower and when you run to him he will keep you safe. Whenever we may feel frightened we can always turn to him and ask for help.

Class work

* Find out how other animals protect their young.
* Talk about people who help and protect us, eg fire service, police force. Brainstorm or prepare a word box or web of 'people who look after me'.
* Think too, of other forms of protection, eg bicycle helmets, seat belts, egg shells, bubble packing.

Special Occasions

31 Harvest: Food for all

Adult or class led

Aim
To show that God has provided food for everybody yet people fail to share.

Bible base
Genesis 1 v29–30. God's twofold provision for human beings and for animals.

Deuteronomy 24 v17–22. God is concerned for the weak in society and commands people to reflect that concern.

James 2 v14–17. Helping the poor. This passage is encouraging us to have concern for the poor, homeless and disadvantaged.

Preparation
There is a lot of material in this outline. Choose which would be most appropriate for your situation.

For the first story attach two spoons to garden canes or poles. Take in some sweets. The story could either be told by the adult with volunteers coming out to help, or members of the class could practise and perform it as a play.

For the second idea take in squash, chocolate biscuits, pretty parcels, cooked rice and water.

Presentation

Tell the children a story about two villages: one called Sunny Side, the other Moaning Meadows. The people in the first one were happy and cheerful, those who lived in the second were miserable. A traveller to the area wanted to know why it was like this so he decided to pay a visit to each place in turn.

First of all he went to Moaning Meadows. On his arrival he saw people looking fed-up and unhappy just as he'd been led to believe. Then he saw why. It was dinner time and they were all trying to eat their food. The problem was they had spoons with very long handles and could not get the food into their mouths. (*Ask some children to try and feed themselves some sweets with the spoon attached to the cane.*) No wonder they were so miserable. They were hungry!

Next he went to Sunny Side. He was surprised to see that they too had spoons with very long handles. However as he watched he understood why they seemed so much happier. They were feeding *each other* using the spoons. They weren't trying to feed themselves, they were looking after each other. (*Children act this out too.*)

The people in Miserable Meadows had enough to eat but they hadn't learnt to share and help each other.

The following could be done as an extra or alternative to the above story.

Ask for some volunteers. Divide the children into two equal groups. For each group choose a child and explain that you are going to help them celebrate their birthday.
Group 1 'Rich Country' – children can be given squash, chocolate biscuits, etc. Wrap up boxes for parcels. Talk about what else you would do at a party and what might be eaten.
Group 2 'Poor Country' – share out a small amount of cooked rice and water (slightly coloured with gravy mix). Talk about whether it would seem like a party with this

food and no presents.

Ask all the children how they could help the children in group 2 to have a good party.

Explain that in some countries people have more than enough to eat, while in poorer countries they hardly have enough or are left without.

Split the children into two groups ready to mime the actions.

Group 1 'You are rich farmers, your crops are growing, the weather is good, you are well fed. How do you feel, look, stand, move?' (*Encourage the children to respond by your example.*)

Group 2 'You are poor farmers, your seeds were good but the soil is poor. How do you feel, look, stand, move?'

Read through the poem and encourage children to mime actions. If they are stuck use the suggested movements given within the text.

1. The following to be mimed by Group 1.
We plough the fields and scatter
The good seed on the land.
(*Pretend to be driving tractors up and down.*)
See the crops are growing,
Aren't they looking grand?
(*All look at each other and nod and smile.*)
We drive expensive tractors,
We fertilize the ground
Then harvest all that lovely food
There's plenty to go round.
(*Pick up imaginary handfuls of food from floor and give to each other.*)

2. The following to be mimed by Group 2:
We plough the fields and scatter
The good seed on the land.
(*Imaginary basket in one hand and throw out seeds with other arm.*)
But we need rain to water it

Our soil is mainly sand.
(*Look up to sky with upturned palms, waiting for rain.*)
We have an ox or donkey
To pull the wooden plough.
(*Some of the children to be animals on all fours while
the others guide them.*)
We have to try and feed ourselves
But never quite know how.
(*Look at soil, shake heads and shrug shoulders.*)

3. *First half mimed by Group 1.*
We sell our crops for money.
(*Half the group sells food to other half who give them
money in return.*)
And spend the pounds we get.
A car, a television
There's lots that we'd like yet!
(*Those who received the money rub hands together and
smile.*) *Mimed by Group 2:*
We never grow enough to eat
We have nothing left to spare.
(*Half the group to go to others asking for food. The
remainder shake their heads.*)
How is it you are richer?
(*Group 2 all look at Group 1 and point.*)
It does not seem quite fair!

4. *All children read/recite together:*
Has God made a bad mistake
About the food supply?
So some of us get plenty
(*Group 1 rub tummies and smile.*)
While others starve and die.
(*Group 2 turn to each other pointing at imaginary empty
bowls.*)
Is there really not enough
In all this world to share?
Or is it that the poor are poor

(*All Group 2 sit on floor.*)
Because the rich don't care?
(*Group 1 turn their backs on Group 2.*)

Ask the children how things could be different? Not having enough to eat is not necessarily the fault of the countries. God has provided enough food for everyone. He knew that there would always be people without food and some who would have more than enough. In the Bible he gave special laws to farmers (Deuteronomy 24 v19) to look after people who didn't have enough. We too can help others who do not have as much as we do.

Class work
* Talk about whether we are a rich or poor country.
* Tell the children about the work of an organisation that is helping the poor, eg TEAR Fund (100, Church Road, Teddington, Middlesex TW11 8QE); Traidcraft (Kingsway, Gateshead, Tyne and Wear NE11 0NE); Oxfam (274, Banbury Road, Oxford OX2 7JF).
* Read other Harvest stories, eg *Miles and the Church Outing*, by Taffy Davies (Scripture Union), 'Norman the Harvest Banana' in *The Reluctant Mole* by Philip Welsh (Scripture Union).
* Tell the children the Aesop's fable 'The Ant and the Grasshopper' where the ants refuse to share their grain with the grasshopper.

32 Harvest: God made it all

Adult led

Aim
To explore the idea that God made everything we need.

Bible base
Genesis 1 v29–30. God's twofold provision for man and animals. The first chapter of Genesis identifies God as the source of all things.

Preparation
Props needed: bar of chocolate, milk, vegetable fat, cocoa, sugar, bowl and Smarties.

Presentation
Show the children a bar of chocolate. How do we get chocolate? We usually buy it in a shop when Cadbury's (or whoever) have made it. Let us see what is in it – milk, vegetable fat, cocoa, sugar. That sounds simple. Let us try and make it. (*Mix all the ingredients together in a bowl. For each of the ingredients trace it back to its origins with the children.*)

Where do we get milk from? Cows. How do they make it? By eating grass. How does the grass grow? In the soil, helped by rain and sun. Who made the sun? God.

We have talked about what we eat but what about what we wear? (*Talk through in the same way the process of making a T-shirt.*)

How about what we watch/do? (*Go through the same process with a video tape or similar.*)

Let us look and see how the chocolate is coming along. (*Ask for a volunteer to come and inspect the bowl.*) It must be more difficult than I think. Good thing I brought along some reserves. (*Share out Smarties with the children if appropriate.*)

Prayers thanking God for the things he has given us.

Class work

* Use the series of books *Thank you for a drink of water* and *Thank you for a pair of jeans* and others (Lion Publishing) to trace other chains of thank-yous.

* See assembly *Ungrateful and Thankful* for further ideas.

33 Harvest: the enormous marrow

Adult and class led

Aim
To show that even our small contribution is enough to change the situation. It is valuable to God.

Assemblies on a similar theme are *The Friendship Cake* and *Hungry and Full*.

Preparation
Props needed: a marrow, simple costumes for Grandad, Grandma, boy, girl, dog, cat and mouse (possibly face paints or masks for the animals).

This assembly could either be led by the adult asking for volunteers or it could be prepared and acted by the class.

Presentation
Bring in a marrow to show the children. Tell the story of the enormous marrow (based on the book *The Enormous Turnip*, Ladybird).

Grandad grew it but couldn't pull it up, Grandma pulled ... boy pulled ... girl ... dog ... cat ... finally mouse and they all fell over as the enormous marrow came up. (*Other characters could be added if more parts are needed.*)

Sit everyone down again.

It was the tiny mouse that made all the difference.

Comment that the little bit that we give can make a big difference. At Harvest we say a big thank-you and we give a little bit back. That makes a big difference to the people who receive it.

That little bit is precious to God.

Class work
* Collect silver paper/stamps/coins for Oxfam.
* Organise a 1p/2p/5p line asking the children to bring in coins on a certain day. Lay them around the hall or along the corridor, or stick on a map of a Third World country. Send the money off to a relief agency.
* See the other assemblies on the Harvest theme for further ideas.

34 Christmas: give us a clue

Adult led

Aim
To help the children understand and know the facts of the Christmas story. To introduce the Christmas story (which some children may have heard several times) in a way that will cover the facts, but keep the children's interest.

Bible base
Matthew 1 v18 – 2 v12, Luke v1–20.

Preparation
Collect a set of numbered envelopes with the following contents:

1. paper ring (representing halo)
2. census form
3. map
4. vacancies/no vacancies sign
5. long strip of cloth, bandage
6. toy sheep
7. picture of someone looking afraid
8. compass
9. paper star
10. gift wrap

Presentation
Distribute the envelopes around the room. Explain to the children that they are going to tell you today's story!

You have got some clues to help them.

Send individual children to find each envelope in turn. When each envelope is opened, question the children to draw the story from them. If you find they don't know the story, you fill it in as far as the next clue.

1. halo – (you may have to hold this over your head to help the children see what it represents). Talk about the angel Gabriel's visit to Mary. What did he tell her? What did she say?

2. tax form – Emperor Augustus ordered that everyone had to go to the town they were born in to be counted so . . .

3. map – Mary and Joseph set off for – where?

4. vacancies sign – but when they got there, there was no room in any of the hotels or B&B's. Where did they go? What happened there?

5. bandage – Mary wrapped the baby in strips of cloth, called swaddling clothes.

6. sheep – meanwhile, on a hillside near the town were some shepherds, staying out all night looking after their sheep. Suddenly . . .

7. person looking afraid – an angel appeared. What did the shepherds feel like? What did the angel say? What did they do?

8. compass – far away in the east, some wise men were setting out on a journey to look for a king.

9. star – How did they know where to go? What happened?

10. gift wrap – when they reached the baby, what did they do?

Conclude by pointing out to the children that all these things don't happen when any ordinary baby is born. Christians believe that Jesus was a very special baby. They believe that he was God's own son, who came to earth to show us how much God loves us.

Finish the assembly by singing 'Mary had a little baby' (*Junior Praise 1*).

35 Christmas: the jolly good news postman

Adult led

Aim
To help the children see that God sent Jesus as a very special present for the whole world.

Preparation
Idea based on *The Jolly Christmas Postman* by Janet and Allan Ahlberg.

Four letters written out on large sheets of paper and four large envelopes containing various things (see presentation).

It may be possible to borrow an actual postman's/post-woman's uniform and a bag for the person delivering the letters.

Presentation
Begin by talking to the children about letters they have received or letters they have sent, perhaps showing them a recent letter sent to you. Discuss letters as a means of communication ... telling people something ... good news, bad news, instructions, etc. Who usually delivers them?

The adult/child acting as the postman should be ready to enter at a given signal to deliver the letter to an appropriate child (eg, a boy for Noah, a girl for Mary etc.) then to exit, and return each time a letter is delivered.

The following script can be used:

Once upon a ____ (day), to ____ (name) school
Came a Jolly Postman looking jolly cool,
With some very special letters.
The first, not for the children, was for Adam and his wife;
A letter, full of good advice from God about their life.

*(Choose an Adam and Eve to open up **Letter 1**. Read it out to the children and discover what is inside.)*

Letter 1: Addressed to Mr & Mrs Adam, The Garden of Eden, The world.
Dear Adam and Eve,
Welcome to my world! I hope you like it as much as I do. Good news! I want you to take care of the world. Enjoy yourselves! I'm so glad I made you.
   With love from God.
(Include in the envelope a picture of a beautiful landscape.)

Continue as the next letter is delivered.

Another letter followed but the news was not all good.
It went from God to Noah and he quickly understood
That all was not so wonderful in God's lovely world,
And rain in showers, torrents, floods, would on the earth be hurled.

*(Choose a Noah to open up **Letter 2**. Read it out and see what's inside.)*

Letter 2: Addressed to Captain Noah, RN, Ararat Village.
Dear Noah,
I expect you've seen that the world is in a mess. I'm really sorry, but I'm going to have to wipe it out and start again. I want you and your family to be safe, so I've put in plans for a special boat you must build.

Yours, very sadly, God.

P.S. The Good News is I promise never to do it again.

(*Include in the envelope plans for the ark, complete with measurements, and a poster of animals to act as a checklist.*)

Continue as the next letter is delivered.

The people didn't seem to learn; they still did what was wrong.

God sent some other warnings too before very long.

He wrote to those who knew him well to see if they could make

The people see some common sense before it was too late.

But nothing, it seemed, would change their ways, so God made a special plan.

He would send his very own son, as a baby to grow into a man.

But who to ask to be his mum? Then Mary came to mind.

Mary was just the right person; loving and gentle and kind.

(*Choose a Mary to open up **Letter 3**. Read it out and see what's inside.*)

Letter 3: Addressed to Mary, 121 Angel Street, Nazareth, Galilee and marked 'Arch-Angel Mail' and 'Special Delivery'.

Dear Mary,

I am sorry Gabriel gave you such a fright the other day, but he's a bright chap and helps me a lot.

I'm really glad that you are going to help me. You're just right for the job.

I'm so excited about this baby. Jesus is Good News for everyone. He will teach them about me, tell them good

stories, make ill people better and be a really good friend.
   Just wait and see how special he is!
   With lots of love, God.
(*Include in the envelope a baby's bib or toy.*)

Continue as the last letter is delivered.

The Jolly Postman brings today one final heavenly note.
God's Good News to all the world: this is what he wrote.

(*Choose a child to open **Letter 4**. Read it out.*)

Letter 4: Addressed to Everyone, The World.
Dear Everyone,
I know you like getting presents. Here's my best ever:
Jesus. He wants to be your friend because, like me, he
loves you very much. That's Good News!
All my love, God.

Continue as the postman leaves.

So the Jolly Postman goes off on his jolly way.
But God goes on forever and with us all he'll stay.
What do you think about him? Will you be his friend?
He'll be yours forever, until the very end.

Finish the Assembly with an appropriate Christmas
song and perhaps a prayer thanking God for the Good
News about Jesus.

36 Christmas – the best present

Adult led

Aim
To help the children think about why we give presents at Christmas.

Bible base
Matthew 1 v18 – 2 v12, Luke 2 v1–20

Preparation
This outline could be used by a team of visitors taking an assembly or as Year 2 class-led assembly. Find a large box to wrap up as a present. In it put a shepherd's head-dress, a toy lamb, a star, a baby doll, and a crown. Have ready some wrapping paper, sticky tape, scissors, and a large bow.

Presentation
Begin the assembly by singing together 'Come and join the Celebration' (*Junior Praise 2*).

Have the box containing the various items on a table at the front and the wrapping paper, scissors, sticky tape, and bow under the table.

One person who will receive the present waits 'in the wings', while one or two people wrap the present and another keeps a lookout for the person coming.

Try and capture the excitement of wrapping presents with the children – 'Won't she/he be pleased with this', etc.

Cut the wrapping paper badly and make some other blunders as you wrap the present hurriedly before the person arrives. The lookout spots the friend coming and the present is given while the others step back looking very pleased with themselves.

The friend unwraps the present but starts to look puzzled and upset saying, 'What is this material? Is it a tablecloth? A cuddly lamb. Oh, a pretty star! I've seen one of these at night-time. It's a nice crown, but a bit big (*tries crown on*). This is a lovely doll, but I've already got one like this (*picks doll up and hugs it*).' As this is said the items are taken out of the box one by one and put on the table.

The recipient of the present stands back. Another person comes on saying that the things in the present weren't what he/she had expected.

Tell the Christmas story using the items in the present (*ask individual children to come out and hold them as you go through*).

The doll reminds us that Jesus was born as a baby in Bethlehem. The head-dress and lamb remind us that ordinary people like the shepherds came to worship him. The star reminds us of how the wise men were guided to Jesus. The crown reminds us that important people (the wise men) also came to see the new baby.

Remind the children that Jesus did not stay a baby but grew to be a man who told everyone about God.

Conclude by asking the children to remember this story when they unwrap their Christmas presents. Jesus came to us as God's present that very first Christmas and is our best present of all.

Finish with a prayer and by singing together 'Girls and boys leave your toys' (*Junior Praise 2*).

37 Christmas: David's party

Class led (probably year 2)

Aim
To help the children remember that Christmas is a time when we celebrate Jesus' birthday.

Bible base
Luke 2 v1–20. The birth of Jesus. Christmas is a time when Christians remember the birth of Jesus, God's son.

Preparation
Talk to the class about times when they have felt left out. Has it ever happened on their birthday? Explain that we celebrate Jesus' birth at Christmas. Sometimes we are so busy having fun that we forget it is his birthday. Practise the play.

Participants: Narrator, father, mother, David, invited children, teacher.

Presentation

Narrator: There once lived a boy called David. He lived with his father and mother in their house in Ware. Soon it would be David's birthday. He was going to be seven.

Dad: It's David's birthday next week, isn't it?

Mum: Yes, let's have a party. I'll invite some of his friends. I'll write the invitations.

David: Oh good, a party. Can I write the invi-

Chief Anderson type
lives on page

	tations, Mum?
Mum:	No, I'll do it. It will be quicker. We'll have Christopher and . . .
David:	Can Simon come, Mum?
Mum:	No, he's too noisy. Come on. It's time for school.
David:	Can I give out my invitations, Mum?
Mum:	No. You'll lose them.
	Here are some invitations to David's party. I hope you can come.
Children	1: Ooh goody, a party!
	2: Thank you.
	3: I hope I can come.
	4: I love parties!
	5: Wonder what we'll have to eat?
	6: I'm going to wear my new jeans.
	7: I think I can go.
	8: I wonder if we'll have crackers?
	9: I'll wear my new shoes.
Narrator:	Everyone was excited about the party, but the strange thing was, no one took any notice of David and it was *his* birthday.
Teacher:	Stand still everyone. Line up. Lead in to assembly. Cheer up, David. It's your birthday next week.
Narrator:	During the day David's mum had been to the shops and bought lots of food for the party. She went to meet David after school.
Mum:	Come on, David. Time to go home.
David:	Is all that food for my party, Mum? Are we having toffee ice-cream?
Dad:	No, I hate toffee ice-cream.
Narrator:	David's mum spent a lot of time getting ready for the party. She worked very hard but she didn't let David help. She didn't even ask him what food he would like. The day of the party arrived. All the children

came. No one said 'Happy Birthday' to David.

Dad: Let's have some games.

Child: Can we play musical statues?

Dad: All right.

Child: Can we play the arches game?

David: Can I be an arch?

Dad: No . . . . and. . . .

David: Can we play musical bumps?

Mum: No. It's time for tea. Everyone sit down.

David: I don't feel hungry. It's a boring party. I think I'll go upstairs and play.

Narrator: No one noticed that David had gone, they were enjoying themselves so much. There was lovely food and games and prizes.

Mum: A present for everyone and it's time to go home.

Children: Thank you very much! Goodbye! Thank you for a lovely party!

Mum: I'm glad that's over for another year.

Dad: Have you noticed something?

Mum: No, what's wrong?

Dad: Where's David?

Comment that David was left out of his party even though it was his birthday. This Christmas let us remember that it is Jesus' birthday that we are celebrating and not leave him out.

Class work
* The children will already be well into thinking about Christmas so it is good to remind them that the reason for the festival is because a special baby was born – God's son.
* Talk with the children about what Christmas means to them. How do they prepare for Christmas? How might they remember Jesus at Christmas time?

38 Palm Sunday

Adult and class led

Aim
To show that Jesus was greeted as a king by the crowds, but he was not the king they were expecting.

Bible base
Matthew 21 v1–11. Jesus enters Jerusalem as a king. Crowds of people were coming to Jerusalem for the great Passover feast. Jesus rode into the city on a donkey but the crowds acclaimed him as a king. There was always the hope that someone would rescue the nation from domination by the Romans.

Preparation
Find pictures and items with a royal theme, eg pictures of the queen, the crown jewels, palaces.

The story of Jesus' triumphal entry into Jerusalem lends itself to drama. Some of the children could prepare palm branches and pretend to be the crowd who saw Jesus going into Jerusalem on a donkey. They can shout 'Jesus is coming! Hooray for the king!' at the appropriate moment.

Alternatively the children could prepare a large frieze of the events.

Presentation
Show the children the royal items. Where do kings/

queens live? What do they do? Have any of the children seen any of the royal houses or a member of the royal family? What do people do when the Queen is coming to town? Tell the children that Jesus was a king and people got very excited one particular day.

Explain that every year there was a special festival called Passover. Jesus and his friends wanted to go. Lots of other people were going too and there was great excitement. Many of the people had heard about Jesus; how he helped others and healed them. They looked up to Jesus as someone special. They thought he was going to help them to get rid of the town leaders who weren't liked or trusted. That was how the procession began.

Jesus wanted to show people that he was a 'King of peace'. He had not come to make war. He chose to ride into Jerusalem on a donkey. He did not have a donkey and so he sent his friends on a special mission to find one. His friends went into town and found a donkey. They told the owner that their master needed it but they would bring it back soon. They took the donkey to Jesus, laid their coats on it and Jesus sat on it.

Everyone was heading for the city. There was lots of noise and bustle, with people calling out to friends and neighbours. When the crowd saw Jesus on his donkey they started cheering. They were so excited that some of them took their coats off and threw them on the ground in front of Jesus. Others broke off branches from the palm trees and waved them. Everyone was talking about Jesus, waving and singing and dancing.

However, some people were going to be disappointed. Jesus was not going to have big armies and fight battles. He wanted to be a king who helped people and taught them to be kind to each other.

Class work
* Read books which tell the story of Palm Sunday from

the viewpoint of the donkey, eg *The Donkey's Big Day* by Gordon Stowell, Little Fish Books, (Scripture Union). The children could retell the story from this viewpoint themselves.

* Bring in some palm crosses. Point out the significance of the symbol of the cross. Children could make their own simple crosses.

* Talk about the different reactions to Jesus among the crowd. Not everyone was happy. Some would have been angry, puzzled, unsure.

* Talk about other celebrations.

39 Easter: new life

Adult led

Aim
To help the children make the connection between the 'new life' symbols used at Easter and the special new life God gave to Jesus.

Bible base
John 20 v1–18. At Easter Christians celebrate the time when God brought Jesus back to life again. They believe that through faith in him, people begin a 'new life' through his spirit.

Preparation
Have ready a daffodil, an egg, a bulb, and a pot containing two bean plants. Prepare six cards with the following words and write the 'responses' on the back of each card:
1. angel – (ting – draw imaginary circle on head)
2. sad – (aaah)
3. garden – (tweet tweet)
4. spices – (rub fingers together and sniff)
5. alive – (hurray!)
6. name – (Mary)

Presentation
Show the children the items one at a time. Ask the children 'What is the same about all these things? What do they have in common?' Talk to them about spring-

time and all the signs of new life. As we come up to Easter we see new life in flowers growing, baby animals being born, chicks hatching, etc.

Tell the children that today they are going to hear a story about a very special new life.

First introduce the cards with the 'key' words written on them. Explain that when these words are said the cards will be held up and they are to join in with the appropriate responses.

Mary is very *sad* as she arrives in the *garden* where Jesus had been buried in a cave. Earlier that morning she had come to the cave to rub some sweet smelling *spices* on Jesus' body but the stone that covered the entrance to the cave had been rolled away and the body was gone!

Mary is so *sad* she is crying as she bends down to look into the cave. As she looks, she sees two *angels* dressed in white sitting where the body of Jesus had been, one *angel* at the head and the other *angel* at the feet. They ask her, 'Why are you so *sad*?' Mary explains that someone has stolen Jesus' body. That's why she is crying.

Then Mary turns round and sees Jesus standing behind her. Through her tears she does not recognise him. Jesus asks her, 'Why are you crying? Who is it that you are looking for?'

Mary explains about the stolen body and pleads with this man (who she thinks is the gardener) to tell her where Jesus' body has been put if he knows.

Then Jesus speaks her *name*. Mary turns to Jesus. He is *alive*! He is *alive*! He is *alive*! She runs back to tell Jesus' other friends that Jesus really is *alive*!

To conclude, talk with the children about the special new life given to Jesus and explain that this is what we are celebrating at Easter.

Finish the assembly with a prayer and by singing, 'God's not dead' (*Junior Praise 1*).

40 Easter: Easter feelings

Adult led

Aim
To familiarise the children with the story of Easter Sunday, showing the change in emotions of Mary in the garden from sorrow to joy.

Bible base
Mark 16 v1–11, John 20 v1–18.
After the crucifixion and death of Jesus, his body was taken down and buried in a tomb. A large stone was rolled across the entrance and the tomb was guarded because of a claim that Jesus would come back to life. On the third day after the crucifixion, the stone was rolled away and people reported they had seen Jesus alive.

This is a fundamental story for Christians. It is important for children to know some of the details if they are to understand how and why Christians celebrate it with eggs, flowers, etc.

Preparation
Buy some hot cross buns and Easter eggs. Prepare a large visual aid of the tomb as shown in the illustration. It should be drawn on card, with the 'stone' made from a separate piece of circular card attached with Blu-Tack.

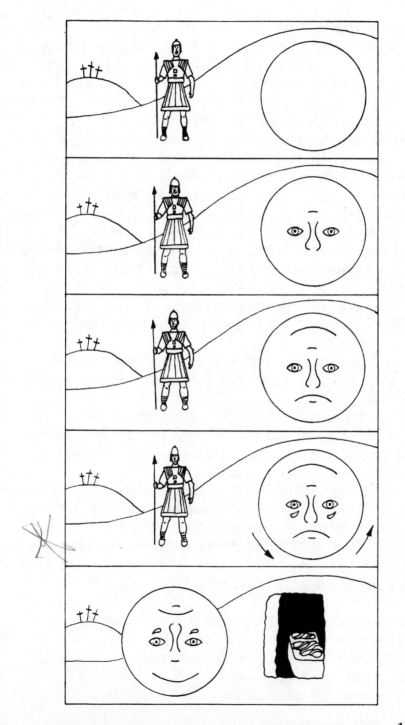

Presentation

Explain that we eat certain things at Easter-time to remind us of certain events. Can the children suggest what? Show the Easter eggs and hot cross buns. Comment that the cross on the buns represents the cross on which Jesus was killed on Good Friday.

Hold up the picture of the tomb. Describe to the children the feelings of Mary and the other women during the three days from Good Friday to Easter Sunday. At each stage, stop and draw with a thick felt marker on the stone of the tomb, so that a miserable face appears stage by stage. When you relate the part of the story when Mary and the other women meet Jesus, roll the stone through 180 degrees, so that the sad face changes into a happy one.

Bring out the following details.

1. Describe what the women saw as Jesus died on the cross.

2. Talk about their sadness as they saw the body of Jesus placed in a tomb and the stone rolled across the entrance.

3. Explain that they went to the tomb on the Sunday morning and how sad they were at the thought of never seeing Jesus again. Mention their fright as the earth shook and an angel appeared.

4. As the stone rolled away, they could hardly understand what was going on. Their fear was changed into joy when they met Jesus and realised that he was alive.

Now draw out the relationship between Easter eggs and the 'new life' which Jesus received when he rose from the tomb on the first morning.

Alternatively the following story could be used:

The empty cave

'We'll never see Jesus again,' the women were crying. 'We thought he'd do so much good and now he's dead.'

They were very sad. Their friend Jesus had been taken

away by soldiers who had led him out of the city to a hill. They had put him on a wooden cross. And he had died. The two women had watched as the soldiers had taken him down from the cross. They saw that a man called Joseph wrapped the body of Jesus lovingly in cloth and carried him to a hollow cave where he laid him. The women had seen how Joseph rolled a big stone over the doorway to the cave.

By then it had been nearly dark, so the women went home. For one whole day they had tried to comfort each other because they thought they would never see Jesus alive again.

Then Mary Magdalene said to the other woman who was also called Mary, 'Let's take some perfume and go to the cave. There was no time to care for Jesus' body before. It's all we can do for him now.'

The other Mary agreed. It was early morning when they set off. Most people were still at home asleep.

The other Mary said, 'I hope we're strong enough to move that big stone so we can get into the cave.'

While she was speaking, the ground trembled under their feet and they fell down. A loud noise rumbled around, like rocks banging and crashing. They covered their ears.

'What's happened?' asked Mary Magdalene when it was over.

'Let's go and see!'

They ran to the cave and stared. The big stone that Joseph had pushed across the doorway had moved. And sitting on the stone was an angel! The women could see into the cave and the body of Jesus had gone!

They were troubled. Had someone else stolen his body? They couldn't understand.

'Don't be afraid,' the angel told the frightened women. 'You came looking for Jesus, but he's not here. This is a place for dead people, but Jesus is alive again. Do you remember he promised that he'd come back to life? Now it's come true!' The two Marys stared into the empty cave. How could Jesus be alive? They'd seen his body taken down dead from the cross. They knew that dead people could not come alive again. They looked at each other.

'But Jesus promised it would happen, I remember,' said Mary Magdalene.

'It must be true!' said the other Mary.

The angel told them, 'Go quickly and tell Jesus' friends. Say that Jesus is alive and wants to meet them. You will see him soon.'

The two Marys were happy, but afraid at the same time. They ran, so excited and full of wonder that they stumbled along, holding each other up because they hardly knew where they were going.

'Is it really true?' asked Mary Magdalene.

'It must be,' replied the other Mary, 'but it's so hard to believe!'

Quite suddenly, they saw a man in front of them. Both together they cried out with joy, 'It *is* Jesus!'

They stopped, still a little afraid, but when they saw his face, they came towards him and fell at his feet. They held him, feeling his warm body, knowing that it was really Jesus. He was truly alive and they were full of joy.

'Jesus – ' sighed the other Mary.

'Don't be afraid,' said Jesus.

The women smiled. Such strange things were happening, but Jesus still loved them, and that made everything right.

He said, 'Go and tell my friends, Peter, James, John and the others to meet me in Galilee. They will see me there.'

Now the two Marys ran on again. They had such exciting news to tell. 'We've seen Jesus!' they told Peter and the others. 'He isn't dead any more. God has brought him back to life!'

Class work

* Make an Easter garden, Easter cards or simple decorated eggs.
* Read the chapter 'Pieces of Howl' in *Haffertee's First Easter* by Janet and John Perkins (Lion publishing).
* Show a life-size cartoon of 'Andy'. The idea is to introduce an imaginary child from a Christian family, then to use him/her to talk about what he learns at Sunday School etc. For this outline discuss what he might do at church on Easter Sunday. What parts of the story make Andy feel sad? happy? Which parts of the story did he find difficult to understand? The 'child' can be used with other stories, eg what songs did he sing at Christmas.
* Other resources – *The Easter story* (Palm Tree Press) and *Lion Children's Bible Series nos. 47 & 48*.

41 Environment week

Adult led

Aim
To show that God wants us to look after the world.

Bible base
Genesis 1. The creation of the world.

The first chapter of the Bible sets out to tell the story of the creation of the world by God. This assembly focuses on God's commission to humankind to look after the world.

Preparation
Props needed: pot plant, plant sprayer and sunglasses.

Presentation
Put some sunglasses on a pot plant and explain to the children that this is George. He is quite a megastar. He has been on Blue Peter and he has made a number of appearances in films, etc. Tell the children the following.

'I am his minder, it is my job to look after him. (*At this point you could spray his leaves, give him some water etc asking one of the children to help you*.) I also keep him regularly fed with Growmore so that he is strong and healthy.

One time after a particularly busy filming schedule I was feeling very tired. I decided that I needed a break and went off on a relaxing holiday. Whilst lying on the beach one day I suddenly remembered that I had forgotten to water George before I went. I dashed to a phone and tried to ring his flat. There was no answer. I rushed to the airport and caught the first plane home. I ran through the front door and there was George. He was looking very weak and feeble and he managed to gasp 'Give me a drink'. I acted promptly and after a while George began to look more like his old self. Of course I felt terrible. I had been very selfish not looking after George properly.'

Go on to draw the parallel with God's creation and how God asked us look after the world.

Ask the children to think about how they might be able to do this.

Say some prayers thanking God for the world and asking for his help to look after it.

Class work

* Talk about ways in which people do not look after the environment, eg litter, pollution etc.

* Look at the story of creation in Genesis 1 and make a frieze.

* Paint some pictures showing the beauty of the world. Also pictures of what happens when we spoil the world, eg what happens when we put rubbish in the sea? What happens when we cut down forests? Underneath write a solution such as 'we could plant more trees, re-use paper'.

* Collect pictures of endangered species and make a book or frieze about them. Find out what is being done to help them. Explain that these creatures are in danger because people have not looked after the world properly and spoilt some of the places where the animals live.

* Look at ways they can improve the school environment.

* Volunteer to keep a small area of the school tidy.

* Grow some seeds/plants and 'look after' them.

Music/Rhyme Resource Books

Junior Praise 1, published by Marshall Pickering.
Junior Praise 2, published by Marshall Pickering.
Ishmael's Family Worship Song Book, published by King's Way Music.
Someone's Singing Lord, published by A & C Black.
Songs For Children, by Ian White, published by Little Misty Music Limited.
Spring Harvest Kids Praise (1988 & 1989), published by ICC.
Children's Praise, published by Marshall Pickering.
Cry Hosanna, published by Hodder and Stoughton.
Let's Join In, published by Scripture Union.